A Memoir

REBEL DOCTOR

From Baghdad to the Australian Bush

Issam Muteir

First published by Busybird Publishing 2018
Copyright © 2018 Issam Muteir

ISBN
Print: 978-1-925692-88-4

Issam Muteir has asserted his right under the Copyright, Designs and Patents Act 1988 to be identified as the author of this work. The information in this book is based on the author's experiences and opinions. The publisher specifically disclaims responsibility for any adverse consequences, which may result from use of the information contained herein. Permission to use information has been sought by the author. Any breaches will be rectified in further editions of the book.

All rights reserved. No part of this publication may be reproduced, stored in or introduced into a retrieval system, or transmitted in any form, or by any means (electronic, mechanical, photocopying, recording or otherwise) without the prior written permission of the author. Any person who does any unauthorised act in relation to this publication may be liable to criminal prosecution and civil claims for damages. Enquiries should be made through the publisher.

Cover image: Dr Zaid Al-Nasiri
Cover design: Kev Howlett, Busybird Publishing
Editor: Allison Duncan
Layout and typesetting: Allison Duncan, Busybird Publishing

Busybird Publishing
2/118 Para Road
Montmorency, Victoria
Australia 3094
www.busybird.com.au

To the spirits of my father, my brother Naeem and sister Saleema.

To my mother; my siblings Saleem, Hakeem, Eklass, Ahmed and Mohammed.

To my wife Jenny.

To my children Yeonju, Maryam and Hadi.

To the sun behind the clouds, that guided me in my life.

To all oppressed people around the world.

I dedicate my book.

To my children Maryam and Hadi,

I am writing these words, not certain if I will be with you, or in a different world when you read them.

When I was a child, my father left the house and never came back. He travelled to a different world. My mother and many others told me that my father was a great person. I had no chance to hear from him, how he had lived and how he had navigated through life. My younger brothers don't even remember what he looked like. They were very little when he died.

I wish I was able to sit down with my father and listen to his life stories. In this life, you can easily lose your loved ones in any moment. I lost both my sister and brother to death at an early age and I am afraid you may also lose the chance to listen to my stories directly from me. I am afraid that there will be a time when you start to ask yourself why your father came from Baghdad, and why he chose to become a refugee in Australia. You may also read or hear from media about Baghdad, Iraq and its wars. You may hear about refugees and may feel embarrassed or ashamed about your roots. I hope not.

The day you came into my life was a turning point for me. I began to think about the future and decided to write down my stories for you and your children. Our origins are important, and this is the memorable story of our family.

My dear Maryam and Hadi, your grandparents were always giving us endless love and taught us valuable lessons so that you in turn can be great people.

As my parent wished for me, I urge you to be always fair, help others, be selfless, be humble and kind. Also, to be proud of your roots, care for your extended family in Baghdad, appreciate what others give you without greediness, and always trust God.

Lastly, I wish you joy reading this book. Always remember that your father loves you.

Issam Muteir, 13th April 2018

Contents

Naeem   i

Part One: Life in Iraq   1
Baghdad   3
My parents   10
Dad's death   15
Culture of fear   17
My first job   19
Naeem and me   19
Understanding Saddam   23
The Gulf War   24
Work at the Presidential Palace   27
Saleema's death   28
The Emergency Force   30
Aiming for top ten in Iraq   31
Naeem and the police   34
University   35
Uday Hussein   37
Military training   38
Elections in Iraq   40
Finishing University   40
Celebrations   42
Working at the hospital   43
No medicines, just corruption   47
Naeem finds trouble   48
Waiting for execution   50
Another execution?   53
9/11   55

Part Two: The Hospital — 57

- Hospital life — 59
- A new relationship — 61
- Escaping Iraq — 63
- Operation Iraqi Freedom — 65
- Cluster bombs — 69
- The authority of one — 70
- Protecting the hospital — 73
- Responsibility of the hospital — 75
- The director's power challenge — 77
- Americans in the hospital — 78
- Mr Prisoner — 79
- Tribal system — 81
- Medicines for the hospital — 82
- Conflict — 84
- After the war — 85
- A trip out — 86
- Handing over the job — 88
- Perilous times on site — 89
- A new force — 91
- The American soldiers — 92
- The new section of the hospital — 97
- Corruption in the hospital — 99
- Explosions at the Holy Shrine — 100
- Iran — 103
- Marriages — 105
- Civil war — 107
- Shi'a bridge — 117
- Working at the clinic — 118
- The Endeavour Scholarship — 119

Part Three: Australia   **131**
    An important meeting   133
    Settling in to Australia   136
    English and medical exams   138
    Life in Albury and making friends   139
    Applying for a refugee visa   140
    Lecturing in neuroscience   142
    Money worries   143
    The immigration interview   144
    A new job   145
    Jenny   148
    Lecturing   151
    Job offer and separation   152
    Warragul Hospital   154
    The medical team from Monash   157
    True ambassador   158
    Leaving Warragul, and beyond   161
    Training in Australia versus in Iraq   162
    Returning to Iraq   163
    Melbourne Western Health Hospital   166
    Reunited with Saleem   168
    More exams   170
    A health scare   172
    Monash 2015   176
    ICU   179
    Palliative care   180
    Learning more from palliative care   181

Postscript   **185**

About the Author   **187**

Naeem

We had no idea how my brother had been executed. Not until later when we saw the thick blue line scoured into his neck.

Death by hanging! A criminal's death.

The same end reserved for murderers, serial rapists, spies and traitors. Naeem was none of them – not even close.

His capital offence? Stealing a few spare parts and selling them.

He was twenty-seven.

Part One:

Life in Iraq

Baghdad

My name is Issam and I am an Iraqi born in Baghdad, Iraq's capital. My birth certificate shows 13 April 1976. However, my mother told me that I was born at the end of the month. Because my father was in the army, the birth certificate couldn't be registered immediately, so we're not exactly sure when I was born. Perhaps I should celebrate every day in April as my birthday.

We were eight – I had three older brothers, one older sister, two younger brothers, and one younger sister. Out of the eight, five of us have university degrees. In those days, it was traditional to have large families. My mother told me she was married at fifteen and, eight years later, my brother Saleem was born. My parents' marriage was arranged and they didn't meet before the ceremony.

My father was born in Iraq's south and had an older sister. Seven days after he was born, his father died. That created enormous financial hardship. Dad, at the age of fifteen, left school and joined the army. Supporting his mother and sister was his priority. When he turned twenty-two, he and his mother went on the pilgrimage to Mecca – a huge achievement back then when most people didn't manage to go until much later in life.

My mother's family lived in the remote southern marshes. The houses were built in the water – a bit like Venice. When she was of schooling age during the 1950s and 60s, there were no schools in the marshes. Only rich people sent their children to school in town.

I didn't realise that my mother couldn't read or write until I was in primary school and I asked her how to say the letter 'Z'. I cried for my mother's embarrassment when I found out she couldn't read.

*

It was 1980, I was aged four. My family and I, along with an uncle, were standing behind the main door of our home. We were looking out at two Iranian jets screaming overhead to attack the city of Baghdad. The planes were flying low: they launched two missiles. I watched them streak into Baghdad and heard the rolling detonations. That night we were all terrified, so my father collected us all into one room to sleep. That day of terror was my very first memory.

The second was of my Uncle Saud, my father's cousin. My father had four cousins – three brothers and a sister. When two of the brothers were at university, they grew up with my immediate family. My father supported them using his army pay so they could graduate. When one of them married, my father helped him move into another home. The third brother, the rich one, was living by himself, and the sister was living with her husband in the same town.

Saud was a very handsome and athletic man. When he finished his business management course, he joined the army as an officer. One day, he came over and cooked sardines with tomato and asked my brother and me to join him. He was very nice and it was a pleasure to eat with him. He had mixed the oil from the tin with the sardines and tomatoes to eat with bread. Delicious! Right then, he looked so full of life. That was the last time I saw him. He went off to the war, and then in September of 1981, the news came to our house that he had not returned, and no-one knew if he had been killed or not.

Everyone came to our house, including the neighbours. I was watching them all crying and talking about Saud. Was he lying dead somewhere? Was he a prisoner of war? My father looked everywhere for him but he was never found.

Uncle Saud (left) at university, 1979.

*

My first day of school was in the first week of October. A week before, I was happily playing near the front door at home when three ladies arrived. 'Are you Issam?' one asked. 'Why are you playing in the mud?' Frightened, I ran inside but they followed me and knocked on the door. They were teachers from one of our three local schools and told my mother that they wanted me for theirs.

My sister went to a school only a hundred metres away from home, whereas my three brothers went to a school only for boys about a kilometre away. The three teachers who signed me up were from the third school – one for boys and girls – and around 800 metres away from home.

On my first day of school, my mother was away so my brother, Hakeem, who was in Year Four, made my breakfast and took me to my new school. It was a strange experience. We were standing around at the school not knowing what to do, with the teachers all talking among themselves. I turned to look at Hakeem, but I saw him waving goodbye as he walked away.

I was in school for about five hours. It was interesting because they gave me books, pens and everything that I needed for lessons. Finding my way home, I found my father waiting for me. He surprised me and greeted me by saying, 'Hello, Doctor Issam'. My father greatly valued schooling and told me that his dream was to see me become a doctor. As young as I was, I never forgot his words. From that day on, I happily travelled the 800 metres to and from school.

I was a good boy in school. In Year Three, the teacher asked the class who wanted to be appointed as a prefect. Everyone in the class raised their hands except me. The teacher came over and asked me why I didn't raise my hand. Telling her I wasn't interested in the role, she promptly informed me that I would be prefect. That was it – stuck with the job until I managed to get myself demoted.

Leaving the classroom one day, the teacher asked me to write down the names of my classmates who were naughty. She had asked me to do the same thing the day before and I had put down five names. That day, I didn't bother writing a new list, I just kept the old one from the previous day. Unfortunately, one of the girls whose name I wrote down was absent and I was found out. A slight miscalculation there. Perhaps I should have realised my potential for taking charge and embraced the job more.

I have to admit I was smart. Although my writing was messy, in Year One I was already reading my brother's Year Two lessons, and I knew the multiplication tables for Year Two. Neighbours would call out, asking me what six times six was, making them laugh when I gave them the correct answer.

In my second year, a boy came to the class from Year Four and said that his teacher wanted me. The teacher had two boys who couldn't answer a subtraction question. The teacher asked me if I could do it, so I did. 'See,' he said. 'A second-year student solved the problem.' I was so embarrassed. I took for granted that the teacher's lessons were easy to grasp, I was surprised that other kids couldn't get it. For me, the lessons all went in and stuck in my head.

I was always eager to go to school. My mother had a lot of children to sort out every morning. The two eldest ones were up at a quarter-to-seven to go to university and I was up at seven for my school. My mother tried to arrange everything for everyone but, with my enthusiasm for my lessons, I'd mess her up by waking up ten minutes too early. 'Sleep!' she would say when she saw my head rise. I just couldn't wait to head off to school.

In my first six years of school, I never missed a day. Mohammad, my friend, would compete with me to get to school first and clean the classroom floor. I left home at a quarter-past-seven, always in a race to get there and get the job done before class started at eight. He was a good friend for three years before he moved away.

Children would be given a *dirham*, around five cents, to buy half a kebab. My mother couldn't afford it and although I accepted that she didn't have the money, I was still jealous. Furthermore, the other children had six nicely coloured pens, and twelve if they came from a wealthy family. I never had any. One of my friends always had money. He was an only child and his father was a high-ranking military officer. He always ranked second or third in exams, whilst I always ranked first.

In Year Three, my mother went to a parents' meeting where the teachers traditionally brought gifts for students who ranked first, second and third. Through a bit of confusion, my mother ended up taking my friend's gift instead of mine. My gift would have been those coloured pens I coveted, instead I ended up with a moneybox. I was terribly disappointed.

I never had to study to remember what the teachers taught us during those first six years. Later in secondary school I worked harder. Nine boys from my street, all from the same soccer team and living in similar situations, went to the same secondary school as me.

*

Every day my mother would cook rice with *margah*, a sort of tomato curry, with meat. It would be paired with different veggies every day. Meat was very expensive so she used about a quarter of a kilo of lamb, dividing it so everyone had twenty to thirty grams. She would put the rice on the plate first, followed by the meat and then pour *margah* over the rice. I was so greedy; I'd often make a hole in the rice, put the meat in and then cover it, telling her that she hadn't given me any. She knew otherwise but would still give me her meat.

A meal like that was very common in Iraqi homes because it was cheap. The rice was subsidised by the government and we usually bought fifty kilos a month. This was one of the few good things about the government at that time. *Margah* was just made of tomato paste and paired with whatever vegetable that was in season – sometimes eggplant, sometimes zucchini – cut into small pieces. From time to time we would get chicken.

All my brothers went to school from eight until twelve-thirty. Lunch, the main meal of the day, was at twelve-thirty; so on the days I went to school from twelve to four, I missed out. In fact, that worked out well because I could eat my meal from the leftovers in the big pot, and there was always lots there.

Did I mention that I was greedy?

*

My sisters and I would help my mother with the housework. Every day during the summer holidays, we would clean the floors with water room by room. The floors were made of stone so it kept the house very cool, and before winter started, we would cover all the floors with traditional rugs and wash them every few weeks.

Summertime was when we would wash all the blankets and floor rugs. There were eight of us so it was a big job. The rugs were four-by-four metres and were very heavy when wet. We would put the rugs on the floor and soak them with running water. After my mother had sprinkled on the detergent powder, I would use my home-made palm-leaf beater to froth up the detergent. One of my sisters would run more water over the rugs until we were satisfied that we had got rid of all the dust and dirt. Then it was time to rinse. Starting at the top of the rug, and, most importantly, using running water and more beating by me, we'd gradually roll it up. It was so heavy. With the help of my brothers, we would carry it outside and drape it over the fence to dry. A couple of days later, it would be dry and light enough for my sister and me to carry it back inside.

As they got older, my sisters helped with the cooking. In Iraq, the daughters usually cook dinner. Lunch was more sophisticated: it was the main meal, so the mums would prepare that instead. Dinner was mainly fried potatoes, fried eggplant covered in oil, or fried onion with tomato. It was a very simple and light meal, easy to make.

*

During my early childhood, the capital, Baghdad, had three overcrowded areas where the poor mainly lived. Displaced people from the south lived there in houses that weren't too bad but, compared to the better socio-economic areas, it was tight, living with ten or more to a household. Bread-winners were usually in the army, or teachers, but their wages were low.

Our house was at the end of town and next to parks, gardens and a tiny river. There was also a farm with all kinds of fruit and vegetables. When school was finished for the day, the other boys and I would go home, throw our bags down, change our clothes, and then go to the park to play soccer. Everyone played soccer – from young boys to sixty-year-old men. Every day, we would play until the sun went down.

Soccer balls were expensive. The other boys and I would pool our money together just to buy a cheap and poor-quality ball. Sometimes the older boys would also lend us their spare ball for a match.

The girls just stayed at home. They would play in the house or on the street in front of the house but wouldn't go out anywhere unless it was with my parents. It was a cultural thing, not religious. My sister played around the house and I would sometimes play skipping rope and hopscotch with her. She also played with dolls. Every season there were particular games that everyone played, and the neighbour's girls would head over to our house to play.

During summer, we would swim. We would also do naughty things like steal the fruit from the orchard. One day, all my friends went to the orchard without me. They stole cucumbers and other vegetables and then destroyed them. The owner saw it and started monitoring the area.

The next day, I went to the orchard with two other friends, not knowing what had happened. The owner ran after us and threw a stone at my head. I heard a *clonk* and felt my head was bleeding but I ran on, escaping to a nearby house where the people there washed and bandaged my head. At home, my father was praying and couldn't be interrupted, but he was watching me very closely. When he finished, he took me to hospital to get six stitches – I still have the scar to this day. He didn't ask me a lot of questions about the injury, but both my mother and father knew I had been naughty so it was left at that. I guess they thought I had received sufficient punishment for my crime.

On some evenings we hunted birds with a slingshot. We did it in the evenings because the birds came down low towards their nests in the trees. One evening, we cooked one of the birds we caught. The next day I got appendicitis. I never ate birds after that.

Bird hunting had a season, just like all the other things we did. For a couple of weeks all the kids in the park would have a slingshot. Then it would be a few weeks of fishing. All our fishing gear was handmade. We would bring sewing needles, put them in a fire until they were very hot, and then bend them into hooks. We would use a piece of sponge as a float to know when a fish was caught on the hook.

During the holidays, I would leave the house at eight o'clock in the morning and come home at eight at night. There was no supervision. Everyone knew everyone because it was a small town and everyone was out playing. Also, my father would only be home five days in a month, and my mother was busy looking after eight kids.

My parents always had to talk to my brother Naeem for being a naughty troublemaker. Concerned, they'd always ask Naeem where he was going during the holidays but they never asked me. He failed the second year of primary school and was always doing naughty things. From a young age, he would escape from school, go to the cinema in the city with a friend, and smoke cigarettes. It was a constant battle for my parents.

*

As a child, nobody would cause me trouble or fight with me because of Naeem. His reputation was so bad that people were afraid of him. It was the law of the jungle, and not being bullied because of him suited me just fine.

However, I didn't get away with it at home. I remembered once when a hat I was fond of disappeared. In my third year of school, I would occasionally get head lice. My mother would cut all my hair off when that happened, and I wouldn't go out unless I wore that hat. I'd even wear it at home and to bed. I woke up one day to find that my hat was missing. When my mother wanted me to buy bread outside, I was upset, searching everywhere for that hat. Crying, I went off to get the bread without it.

When I got home, the whole family were seated around the remains of my hat. Hakeem had burnt it. We all laugh about it now, but I was inconsolable for days. Back then, Hakeem was always mean to me.

As a boy, I liked to read the newspaper and follow the news about the Iraqi soccer team, who were doing well during the 80s. Hakeem would buy the newspaper every day but wouldn't allow me to read it, telling me to buy my own. If I touched it, he would shout at me and hide it.

However, outside the house nobody would touch me, not only because of Naeem's reputation, but because I was wise and smart, and people trusted me. Without fail, I told the truth and I was honest. If my friends wanted to go swimming or play and wanted someone to look after their valuable items, they trusted only me.

*

In my sixth year of primary school, my English teacher decided that everyone who was good at their studies should teach five of their fellow students who were struggling. The students would come to the park with me for a few hours after school on Fridays where I would teach them before we played soccer. I was happy to do that but, after a while, my mother went to the school and complained. The school stopped asking students to do it after that.

In Year Eight I started teaching officially. In Year Seven and Year Eight, if we had average marks above 85 percent in the first and second semester exams, we didn't have to sit through the final exam. I was the only one who didn't have to study after March, while the rest of the students continued until June and I taught.

That became the pattern for the rest of my high school years.

My parents

My mother was very hard working. While looking for ways to make enough money to supplement Dad's army pension, she would go to Baghdad's main market, buy clothes for kids, nappies and sewing material and then sell them in our hometown. She supported us a lot and is a great woman.

She was always quiet and patient. She never shouted at us and always tried to make something from nothing. For example, with the small amount of black bread that was supplied, she divided it evenly and said, 'That is for you, and that is for you'. We understood that things were tough, and she was trying her best to provide for us in a wise manner. Throughout all the hardship, she never gave up or became frustrated. She just got on with it.

Her ambition was to get us through university.

*

Because he was a career soldier, Dad wasn't around home much. And when he was, being allowed five days off a month including travelling, he was out making money by providing an unofficial taxi service. It was the sort of thing many men did if they had a car.

When it was Dad's day for coming home, we'd get very excited and, knowing that his bus arrived around three in the afternoon, we would stand on the bed nearest the window and watch the bus stop in the street.

A bus would pull up, and we'd all hold our breaths for Dad's big army bag to clump onto the road. Then, someone would shout, 'Aha, Dad is here!' Then we knew he'd arrived and we'd all scamper to the door to open it for him.

Then off he'd go in his car the next morning. He was a terrible driver and often had accidents. Due back home around two or three for lunch, sometimes he'd be very late, and we knew that he'd probably hit something with his car. This made us sad because he'd often put all us kids in the car when he came home and take us to a falafel shop to buy us food. He'd buy a falafel between two of us, and we'd sit down in the street to eat. If he'd had an accident, that wasn't going to happen.

My father, a very religious man and always praying, was very popular with neighbours and relatives who'd all visit when he was home. He had a good sense of humour and would tease my mother, telling her that he'd get a second wife when he retired. Mum pretended to be upset, but she knew he'd never do such a thing.

One day, I had severe abdominal pain. It was over a kilometre to the hospital gates, but my father didn't hesitate, hoisting me onto his shoulder and carrying me all the way there. By that time, I was quite heavy too.

Later on, when I was twelve I developed appendicitis. We didn't know it at the time, and my father wasn't home, so Mum took me to hospital. When the doctors came to examine me, she'd disappeared somewhere. Pressing on my abdomen, the doctors told me that I needed an operation and when I asked what would happen if I didn't they said, 'Something terrible will happen to you.' I was asked to sign a consent form, but before I did I asked them for details about the operation – you see, I was already a budding doctor.

My mother still hadn't appeared when it was time to take me to the theatre so off I went. I remember that a nurse was laughing at me, pointing me out because my underwear was a pair of cut down pyjamas. I would often play soccer around the yard at home without bothering to change out of my sleepwear, so the knees of my pyjamas became shredded. Rather than throw them out, Mum would cut them off at the knees and get some use out of them. This sight caused great hilarity among the surgical staff who had never worried about getting the most out of clothes.

When I woke up, my mother had re-appeared. I can't remember where she'd been, probably trying to contact Dad.

I was released from the hospital after three days and allowed home. Dad arrived around the same time carrying an enormous bag of apples for me from the north – a real treat as apples weren't obtainable in Baghdad. He took the biggest apple out of the bag and said, 'This is Issam's.'

My father was a kind person. He was short, had a moustache and was always smiling. He always tried to use the formal Arabic language with us, which was funny because we would use slang instead. He was a smart man and always encouraged our education because he missed his chance to continue formal studies. He loved us and people admired and liked him a lot because he was so giving. Our father was different from all his peers because of his generous nature.

Someone told me that one day my father visited his uncle in hospital and noticed that his underwear was very dirty. My father was wearing new underwear so he went to the bathroom, took off his underwear and changed my uncle's. That was just one example of my father's kindness. No one else would think to do that. Can you imagine such kindness? I was proud of him.

He was not good with us in one way, though. His rich cousin lived close to us and had a son Hakeem's age. My father would buy sports shoes for Hakeem, and at the same time buy some for his nephew even when he hadn't asked for them. My father would always give his nephew what he asked for but he didn't always do the same for Hakeem. He would be kind and show love for others even if he had to cut back on his own family. It's an Iraqi tradition where the extended family is a priority.

My father hit me only once. In September 1986, we were celebrating *Ashoura*, a religious festival which commemorates the death of the grandson of Prophet Mohammed, who went into a battle at Karbala in which he and his family were killed. The difference between Shi'as and Sunnis is based on this event and Saddam, being a Sunni, was against the festival and banned it. Despite that, we still celebrated *Ashoura*.

Traditionally, everyone stays up all night cooking food which is then given to others. Naeem and I joined a group of about twenty walking to a Shi'a holy shrine about an hour from home. This was dangerous because Saddam had forbidden visits to the shrines and would punish or even execute anyone who went. If my father had been home he would have stopped us, but he was away with the army – or so we thought.

We reached the shrine at about three-thirty in the morning and I was amazed. The shrine was made of gold and had many mirrors; it was a dazzling sight to a youngster like me. We prayed there and left.

That day, my father had just been released by the army and arrived right after we left the house. He was frightened for us and couldn't sleep because he knew Saddam and understood what could happen to us. When we told him we'd been to the shrine, he slapped both our faces. I fell to the floor in shock and remained there. My father then left the room, locking the door behind him. It was a very small room and it felt like being in prison. I was still on the floor when he came back later and, without saying a word, unlocked the door and went away.

I left the room and went up to the roof. During the summers, we slept on the roof to stay cool. As I walked to my bed I saw my father fast asleep. That was the only time he ever hit me, and we never talked about it.

My father was bitterly disappointed with Naeem for his bad behaviour and poor school record. As his own family was poor growing up, my father never had the opportunity to continue his education. Despite that, he was able to provide everything for us: a home, food, and everything we needed to study. He always told us, 'You study because it's your weapon, and if you don't have a weapon, you die.' So Naeem was always being punished. My father would tie him to a tree for an hour or throw him into the sewage.

But it didn't help. Naeem was Naeem.

*

The marshes where my parents lived had plenty of water, like a lake. One of the plants growing there was used for constructing handmade houses. Over time the district became renowned for being anti-Saddam, so Saddam restricted the water to the area, drying the land, and forcing everyone to leave.

Today, due to its world heritage listing of the site, UNESCO has committed to bringing the marshes back to life. The animals have returned and people are living there again. The people live entirely on the water, moving on boats between dwellings and they depend on the fish and birds for food. There are also small areas to keep cows for milk. It's a simple and environmentally friendly life.

When my father was in the army, the family moved from one place to another. First my parents moved to Diyala, east of Baghdad, where my eldest brother and sister were born. Then the family moved to the south to Basra where my two brothers arrived. In 1976, before I was born, my father was posted to Baghdad. He was a non-commissioned officer and maintained that rank throughout his career.

We were regarded as a poor family because Saddam was paying my father about 180 Iraqi dinars, which is only about AU$100 to $150 per month. Eight children! All of us students! He gave half the salary to my mother and kept the rest because he needed to support himself in the army.

My mother had to borrow money for food from my uncle. When my father came back home with his salary, my mother would pay back the debt. We were unable to afford anything. My father would be with us for only five days each month, so my mother would constantly be in my uncle's debt. That uncle was rich, as his father worked in Kuwait earning a lot of money and sent large amounts back to him.

Saddam Hussein was in power for thirty years, and because of the war between Iraq and Iran from 1980 to 1988, he did not allow military personnel to retire. However, at the end of the war, he decided that anyone with thirty years of service had to retire. My father had never seen active service. In 1985, he was punished for a minor transgression and sent to the freezing north for five years. Because of the extreme climate, it was a posting that was loathed and feared by all military personnel.

On 26 October 1989, my father finished his service with the army. He came back from his posting near the Turkish border to be with us for one week before returning north as a civilian to submit his retirement papers. He took the train.

There was an accident.

He did not survive.

Dad's death

According to my mother, while my father was in the army in 1985, he was posted to Baghdad. He would come and go from home every day. It was also well known that he took religion seriously, he was always praying. He was a Shiite, the oppressed majority which Saddam Hussein discriminated against.

My father was against the government and always called the Socialist Ba'ath party, Saddam's political party, *Halaku*. *Halaku* was a Mongol who invaded Baghdad in 1258 and was famous for destroying the city and throwing all the books into the river.

My father's constant praying upset members of Saddam's party. Sensing that he opposed them, they punished my father by sending him to the north. It was a terrible place to be. Often, soldiers disappeared, captured by the rebels and killed.

I didn't hear these details about my father until twelve years after his death. Working in the medical ward of the Saddam Heart Surgery Centre, I became aware that many of the patients were VIPs from Saddam's party. I was informed one day that one of my patients was from that group, so I decided to treat him last.

The nursing staff also disliked treating Saddam's party because making a mistake could cost you your life.

I finally went to my last patient. I was nervous and tried to avoid looking at him. He asked me if I was Mr Khuleif's son and, surprised, I told him that I was. He said that he had known my father in the army and worked with him. The patient, who turned out to be one of Saddam's relatives, told me that he was the leader of the Ba'ath party back then and had ordered my father to stop praying and to stop calling them *Halaku*, confirming what my mother had said. I quickly told him that I knew nothing about it, that I was just a kid back then and hardly knew my father.

The day my father died, we heard on the television that three carriages of a train going north had slipped into a valley. The rails had collapsed and there were two hundred people killed or injured in the accident. We suspected that it might have been the train my father was on, but couldn't be sure.

We heard nothing about my father for about a week. One of our relatives saw our father's name on a list of the dead at the train station. Talking it over with Saleem and Hakeem, they decided not to tell the rest of us, but to go north in my father's car to find him. All our relatives knew our father had been killed except us. Hakeem was only sixteen and Saleem twenty-one – so young for such a responsibility.

It was a winter's night and around eight o'clock an uncle came to the house and stayed past eleven when everyone wanted to sleep, which was a bit strange. We found out why when the car returned with my father in a coffin. Opening the door, we realised what had happened and my mother fell to the ground crying. We brought my father's body inside, keeping him in the house until morning. All my uncles and their families arrived and nobody slept that night.

Funerals in Iraq usually last for three days. We put up a big tent at the front of the house and people came from the town and the south of Iraq. The southerners stayed with us the entire time. The tent was huge so everyone could sit in it and pray, read the Quran, and conduct religious ceremonies. I remember that it was terribly cold.

I couldn't talk to anyone for two days because I was too shocked. I just sat at the end of the tent watching, until my granduncle came and sat with me. 'Oh, my son, Issam,' he said, 'you know your father has died and now you need to move on and you need to help your brothers.' My brothers were very busy serving the people who had come to visit. My granduncle said I should be helping rather than sitting there being sad. I started to help and when the funeral was over, I went straight back to school.

As my father was submitting his retirement papers when he died, we could not get any money for nine months. The Iraqi military required that retirement papers be presented in the place of the last posting, which was why my father had to return to the north. Someone from the family had to go north to complete the retirement papers.

My mother asked her brother to go for her. With Hakeem, who was only sixteen, they made the 400-kilometre trip. It was a dangerous drive through the mountains, followed by poorly paved roads.

The nine months of waiting for the paperwork to be approved was a very hard time for us all. Hakeem and our uncle had to ask for money for the travel. We were all students, so my mother borrowed money from my uncle.

I don't know how my father had managed that trip every month for years. He had a hard time but never complained.

My father.

Culture of fear

When I was in Year Five, one of my close friends was Kasim, who had an older brother in the Communist Party. Saddam had the brother arrested in 1981 but his family didn't know what had happened to him or where he was. I remember Kasim telling me about his brother being taken, but the rest of the family wouldn't talk about it. Then, in 2003 when America invaded Iraq, he discovered that his brother had been executed in 1985.

I had another friend at school, Maithem, whose older brothers, Saad and Raad, were in the Islamic Party, *Al Dawa*. They were executed in 1981. My neighbours had one son killed in the Iran War and a second became a prisoner of war. Everywhere around us, lives were being lost. Political accusations meant you would lose your life;

being in the war meant you would probably die. In the 1980s, we were all too young to be in the army; yet, we still lost Naeem.

Everyone in the town was affected and everyone had lost someone. Saddam had created a culture of fear. Just walking around the town could mean being arrested and sent to the police station.

*

Where we came from, if we failed three years of secondary school, we would be sent into the army – a terrible fate. In 1990, I was in Year Eight and many students in my year had already failed once or twice. They were afraid to try again, despite the fact that they didn't work hard at all. I couldn't understand why they didn't make the effort to stay out of the army.

The teachers, too, were in a quandary. They had to be strict and not give a pass unless the marks had actually been achieved. They knew failed students would be sent to the army and would probably die in the war, but falsifying grades could also get them punished.

I really cared about other people and was always a good listener. Although I studied hard, I was friends with everyone and was not nerdy and isolated like how some bright students could be. In fact, I was a leader, both in sport where I was captain, and in our gang.

One guy, Ali, was four years older than me and had failed for the second time. We became good friends, so I helped him cheat. Sitting behind me in the exams, I would signal the answers to the true or false questions by raising one hand or the other. I wanted him to avoid the army.

I helped Ali to pass. He gave me a gift of a very nice silver ring, a fashionable item for young boys.

Unfortunately, when Saddam invaded Kuwait, the government decided that failing two years of high school meant being sent to the army. Despite our efforts, Ali was conscripted and after the war I heard that he had been killed, along with so many others.

Life was tough at that time. We lost friends and neighbours – people were dying all around. That is what was happening around me, right through primary school and high school. I survived, but my experience made me angry and I realised the need for change.

My people deserved better.

My first job

During the holidays from 1990 to 1991, I started working in a factory from eight in the morning, and spent twelve hours cutting plastic for making nappies. I was thirteen years old; it was after my father had died. I was responsible for packaging the nappies after they were sewn. I continued with this job until I started my degree.

When I started working at the factory, the owner's son had just failed Year Nine English. I was asked to tutor him from eight until twelve each morning, and then I would work in the factory until eight at night and was paid the same money. In Iraq, we learnt English from Year Five. His son didn't even know the English letters. He really didn't know anything after five years of learning and the exam was very tough. For some reason, students' inability to learn English was very common in poor areas. In my class I would get ninety percent, but the next closest student would only get forty-five or fifty.

Rather than proper teaching, I taught the student how to just answer the questions. I used repetition and told his father that I would drum enough into him to get fifty to seventy percent. He got sixty-seven after only three months.

One day, after finishing work, the owner of the factory walked with me from the city to my house because he lived nearby. He said to me that study wouldn't get me anywhere so he would teach me how to operate a machine at the factory. In my heart, I knew he wouldn't. I had been reading about capitalism and understood that many business owners just used their workers.

A neighbour had worked in that factory for many years, but the owner wouldn't teach him how to sew. The owner believed my neighbour would learn the tricks of the trade and then go off and work for himself.

I knew not to leave my studies: that was my understanding of the world when I was twelve and thirteen.

Naeem and me

Because Naeem was always the naughty one, he was considered to be a brave boy. He usually was, until it came to suffering pain, especially when it was going to involve his penis.

Traditionally in Iraq, boys are circumcised around the age of two or three when they're unaware of what's going to happen, and don't have any later memory of the procedure. Unfortunately, with Dad being away in the army, Hakeem, Naeem and I missed out until much later. Hakeem would often tease us, saying that he'd take Naeem and me to get the scissors, but when it was his turn, he ran into the garden and climbed a tree refusing to come down.

I was around ten, and Naeem twelve, when Saddam decreed that all the hospitals were to open their doors for free circumcisions to commemorate the 1958 revolution. My father was home at that time, so he bundled my uncle, Naeem and myself into the car and carted us off to the nearest hospital to take advantage of the deal.

Unsurprisingly, the hospital was a madhouse. Hundreds of people were milling around trying to get free circumcisions for their boys. It was a joy to see. Naeem and I knew we wouldn't get our procedures done that day.

We were wrong. My father wasn't about to give up on a free offer and drove to the next nearest hospital. It was the same situation, and we breathed another sigh of relief. Wouldn't we surely go home now?

But my father was a determined man, and on we went to the third hospital. It was almost as bad, but my father decided that we would wait. Eventually, we were taken to a room with two beds. Naeem and I were held down by our arms and legs. We struggled but could hardly breathe, never mind move. It was a terrifying moment. Why would we be held down so fiercely unless something horrible was about to happen?

We saw the enormous scissors. There was no anaesthesia, so we knew it was going to hurt like hell. The doctors put an instrument over the foreskin to stretch it out. We both shrieked with the terrible pain. It felt like my heart was coming out of my throat. God, it was awful. I was crying out for my mother, 'Mum, Mum, Mum!' and Naeem was screaming out, 'Daddy, Daddy!'

In a way, it was hilarious because here was the tough, strong Naeem reduced to a blubbering child when everyone thought he'd be resilient and stoic about it all. At that point, I decided to keep quiet and be the dignified one and let him do the crying for both of us. And he took centre stage with his performance.

Snip and slash, it was over. We were taken home, put into beds together and given lollies. Because of the wounds, we had to be careful to keep clothing off our penises. Even so, it was still painful, and we couldn't do anything much for a few days. Despite that, it was a time for celebration when friends and family visited us with more lollies and gifts. It wasn't so bad after all.

Naeem was teased relentlessly for years for crying like a baby. He took it well enough – most of the time.

*

Naeem was very keen on breeding birds, and had an aviary on our roof. It's a common hobby for boys and men in Iraq and quite a little business. The practice is looked down on because it's assumed that time spent on the birds and making money is time not spent studying. In Naeem's case, that would be spot on.

The birds are like brightly coloured homing pigeons, trained to learn where their home is and return from many kilometres away. A neighbour's birds which may lose their way or follow your birds and end up in the wrong aviary are considered fair game and will be sold or exchanged at the bird market. It's an on-going war.

The birds are also expensive, particularly those that can do acrobatic tricks. Naeem's flock of seven birds was valuable, so when he asked me to look after them one summer when I was nine years old, I was very nervous.

Naeem had recently cut the birds' wing feathers so they couldn't fly away until they learnt where their home was. He trained me how to look after them, teaching me the birds' names, how to feed and water them, and how to buy their food. I was also responsible for placing a pot of water in their cage every afternoon, so they could swim.

I took my duties very seriously, and I was proud that my brother had entrusted his precious birds to me for safekeeping. So, imagine my distress when one of them, a beautiful white one, died on the very first day of my guardianship. However, it turned out well because the white one had been partnered with a red bird called Bukhari, who then partnered with another bird who laid some eggs. I was tremendously excited and watched every day to see if they hatched.

Just before Naeem was due back, I took the water upstairs for the birds to have their swim and placed the bowl outside the cage. Out they came for a dip and then unexpectedly flew on top of the cage. I was horrified. That wasn't supposed to happen. Taking a broom, I tried to coax the birds back into the cage. Then three of them, Naeem's pride and joy, flew away.

Stricken with shame and disappointment, I sat in the stairwell and wept. I was sobbing so loudly that Hakeem and my sister, Saleema, came up to ask me what was wrong. I was wailing and so distraught that I could hardly speak. And then Naeem came home.

'Issam, Issam, why are you crying?' he asked. 'All your birds have gone,' I howled. 'They've all flown away.' Naeem laughed and went up to the roof. I couldn't believe it. Here was a tragedy of enormous proportions and all he did was laugh at me.

'Issam, Issam,' he called. 'Come up here and look.' With heavy feet, I went to the roof afraid to see. And there were all the birds, happily back in their home. I had forgotten that they were programmed to come back once they learned where their home was.

Naeem was also delighted that there were eggs. They eventually hatched which pleased my brother even more, because up until then he had acquired birds either at the market or from the bird war.

My brother developed quite a reputation for being a tough guy. People were either afraid of him or at least respected him. When I was in Year Eight of secondary school, I went to buy a newspaper near home during the holidays, two much older boys tried to bully me. Because it was two against one, I decided not to fight. They were about to hit me when I saw a neighbour, an old man, and called out to him for help. The man came over and told the boys to leave me alone and then took me home. I couldn't wait for the holidays to be over so I could get one of the bullies on his own back at school.

Sure enough, on the first day back, I caught him in the playground and reminded him of the previous encounter. 'Now we're man to man,' I told him. 'You don't have your friend to help you bully me.' With that, I grabbed his neck and punched him in the face until his nose bled.

Just as the gathered crowd was pulling us apart, Naeem came walking over with some friends. He walked like a cowboy in the *High Noon* movie, with a confident swagger, even though he was shorter than me.

Everyone, frightened of Naeem, fell silent and waited for him to speak. 'Why are you fighting, Issam?' he asked. 'Why are you hitting this guy?' I told Naeem about everything that had happened.

He turned to the boy, looked at his bloody face and said, 'Don't you ever come near Issam again, or speak to him!' The boy was terrified, and I had my revenge.

That was my brother, Naeem. He had a presence, and he had an air of menace. Nobody wanted to go against him, and he didn't have to fight anyone because he had an air of absolute authority and charisma. He was strong-minded and would never show sadness or emotion, always in control of himself and the environment. When things went wrong, he'd say, 'Don't worry, all will be fixed.'

Although quite different, he and I were close as children and then regained our friendship later when I was in medical school. He would call me, and we'd go to a lovely riverside restaurant with our little brothers and have some fine food, and he'd smoke a shisha. I think he found peace there with me. I believe he was also sick of being with people he couldn't trust. Because I was a student, he'd pay for everything which was a treat for me.

I miss him.

Understanding Saddam

In August 1990, Iraq invaded Kuwait. At the time, we were sleeping on the roof because it was summer. At nine in the morning, my sister woke me up. Holding a radio, she told me that it had happened. My brothers and I went down to turn on the television to watch the invasion. We had no idea what was going on.

The news stated that there was a revolution in Kuwait and the people had asked Iraq for help. That was not true, but we didn't know it at the time. My family didn't trust Saddam, always listening to him with suspicion. In the evening, my brother switched over to Voice of America because we knew Iraqi television didn't always tell the truth.

Voice of America gave us a completely different story. The United Nations Security Council and the rest of the world were condemning the invasion. The next day, Saddam decided to withdraw from Kuwait and then changed his mind again, deciding that Iraq and Kuwait should be one country.

It was unlawful to listen to Voice of America and other radio stations like Radio Monte Carlo and BBC. If we were caught listening to those stations we could be executed, but most people listened anyway. We would just go inside the house away from the street and tune in.

When I was growing up, I read all of Saddam's books. Everything was from the perspective of the Ba'ath party. They would talk about capitalism and the communist party, how they were wrong, and how only the Ba'ath doctrine was correct. Because I was a child, I believed what was said, as well as the media announcements. With the invasion, I lost trust in the television because I could see more than one reality. I began to understand that Iraqi television and Saddam's books were not the truth.

I was fourteen and the revelation that all wasn't what it seemed was a terrible shock to me. I believed in Saddam and believed what he said. An uncle in the Iraqi army hated Saddam and called him *Abu Haiwan*, 'the father of the animal', a very insulting term. When he discovered me listening to Saddam on the radio, he was disappointed in me and asked me why I was listening to the father of the animal.

I also had a neighbour, Salah, who was an old man in the army. I was sitting with him one day defending Saddam. He gave me examples of what Saddam was doing but I continued to support him. I was defending the doctrine rather than what was happening in the real world. When I started to listen to the Voice of America, that all changed for me.

In 1991, after the war, many people were executed. I knew then, at just fourteen, that Saddam was bad. My family didn't openly discuss Saddam, even though they loathed him. Just talking about the man could get people killed. My uncle and the neighbour were the only people who would talk to me about Saddam, and it wasn't until I was about seventeen that I could talk about Saddam to a friend.

When I was in primary school, I knew a very smart girl called Intisar (which means 'victory' in Arabic) and her brother Ahmed, who was two years older than us. They lived in a house on the way to school and Intisar's father was a driver between Baghdad and Jordan. Suddenly, the entire family was gone and the house was empty.

We knew Saddam had taken them but didn't know why. We pretty-well knew they had been executed.

The Gulf War

On 17 January 1991, at two-thirty in the morning, the Gulf War started. The sounds of missiles and aircraft roared around the house. It was frightening. Sitting together in the same room, we shivered in fear of a chemical or nuclear attack and didn't sleep. In the morning, my mother decided that we should leave Baghdad and go south to where my ancestors lived. Piling into a neighbour's car – they were also escaping – we joined the huge swarm of people and traffic fleeing out of the city. The roads were so jammed that it took hours to get away.

We went to my uncle's house first but as they had no food, they couldn't put us up. Apart from that, there were many military installations in the area that became missile targets. We then went to look for my mother's sister. My aunt was quite well off and was living in Al-Fuhud, a small town in a remote area in the south. The rural towns saw fewer missiles.

However, we were four families staying in one house – more than forty people. There was no electricity and everyone had to sleep in the main living room. After two weeks, the food ran out and, with the aircraft and missile attacks increasing, we decided to return to Baghdad. However, that was not easy.

Our first attempt wasted an entire day waiting at a garage for a lift. Not only was there no fuel, as the Americans had bombed the petrol stations, people were too afraid to go to Baghdad. Now we had two enemies, Saddam and the US.

Eventually, Naeem, who was sixteen at the time, told my mother that he was going back alone. He jumped into a truck going to Baghdad and left. We returned to my uncle's house, deciding to split into two groups the next day. Leaving my sister and my brother Mohammed with my uncle, Mum, Hakeem, my younger brother, Ahmed, and I went back to the garage. Managing to squeeze onto a truck with many others, we sat on the floor for six cramped and uncomfortable hours until we arrived in the city.

At home, we found that tricky Naeem had arrived the day before, managing to break into the house by jumping from a neighbour's roof onto ours. On the way to our house we saw people, including my friends, at the park playing soccer. Realising that things weren't so bad now, Hakeem went south the next day and brought back the rest of the family.

Every evening at seven o'clock the attacks started. It became a routine. The attacks would stop the next morning and things would almost return to normal.

There was one night when a small nearby airport was under attack all night. Our house was shaking with each missile and bomb. Doors and windows were shaking with very scary sounds. We were lying in one room, and no one was able to sleep. There was no electricity, no lights. We couldn't see each other in this darkness but I could sense the fears in the voices of my sisters and brothers.

As always, my mother was trying to keep us calm. She was reassuring us that everything would be alright. I managed to close my eyes just after 5 am.

During the day time, we had different struggles. My mother and I would go to the small river close to our house and bring water. I would also cut trees with my friends to bring home wood needed for cooking.

*

The war ended on 28 February 1991, but the Iraq opposition then began a rebellion against Saddam. In the north, there was also a revolution by the Kurds. We waited for the rebels to arrive in Baghdad but it didn't happen because the US allowed Saddam to attack them.

He attacked the south and the Kurds in the north. About 300,000 people died. Two million people escaped through Turkey and another million escaped south to Iran. Saddam was merciless, grinding us under his boots until there was no opposition left to fight him.

Day by day, Saddam fixed up the infrastructure. Electricity came back, the radio and then the schools started again. He called it 'Reconstruction'. Along with all the boys in our town, my brother Hakeem and I were given work, and money was printed to pay us. During the holidays, I carried damaged stones to a truck to be transported elsewhere. I also had a second job working in a hotel at the airport removing the wallpaper so that the walls could be painted. That was a nicer job – easier and a bit of fun.

At first, the flood of newly printed money was fine, but a year later what would have cost five dinar was 250 dinar. Before the war, one dinar was worth three US dollars, but later, one US dollar bought 200 dinars. It was rampant inflation, not helped by UN sanctions that lasted thirteen years. Iraq was not allowed to export oil so we were unable to obtain food or medicine.

The worst year was 1993 because we had little sugar, rice, or flour. Saddam started 'Distribution'. Every month each family would be given a certain amount of rice, sugar, flour and oil depending on the number of people in each household, and the price would be subsidised. At least people could get food. Every month we bought a quarter kilo of sugar, one kilo of rice per person – the minimum a person needed to survive. It was a tough year.

Saddam had the impression that the merchants were cheating, but they were just buying and selling. He became enraged and executed twenty of them.

As the years went by, Saddam increased the allocations and used the flour meant for animal feed to make black bread. The supplies were never enough and the extra kilos of rice we needed gobbled up an entire month's salary.

My mother only had one ring from my father but she had to sell it to buy sugar and rice. She also had to sell the television and most of the furniture. One day, Mohammed was sick so my mother and Naeem took him to the doctor. She was given a prescription but had no money to get the medicine. That affected Naeem's attitude greatly.

Work at the Presidential Palace

I wanted to make a book about the 1990 Soccer World Cup, so I collected newspapers that had pictures of all the best players, including the players from Argentina and Germany. Planning to arrange the pictures into a small book and write something about the Cup, I needed a copybook for the project. I had no money so I joined my friends who were working on war damage at the Presidential Palace where Saddam and his son, Uday, lived. Although it was very hard work carrying stone from one place to another, it was a still a very interesting day.

We were taken in a truck from one side of the palace to the other, and saw Uday's quarters with a lovely swimming pool and bar. The grounds were beautifully manicured with well-established trees everywhere. Although we didn't see either Saddam or Uday, it was an opportunity to see a beautiful part of Baghdad. It was a different world entirely, and a sharp contrast to the town I was going back to: unable to afford a mere copybook, and knowing that there were people in prison for nothing, or hard workers being paid the equivalent of just three dollars per month.

Why did we have to suffer? At thirteen, I didn't understand, but I kept thinking about it, trying to make sense of it all – and keeping those dangerous thoughts to myself, of course.

Saleema's death

In 1993, Saleema was in her final year of a teaching degree at university and went for a placement in a school. On her first day at school she had a serious asthma attack and came home. That same day, she went into hospital and died.

Exactly forty days before, I'd had a fight with her. She was still wearing black to pay respect to my father who had passed away four years previously. Usually, women wore black for only one year after a death. Saleema told my mother and me that she now wanted to buy white clothes and had been dreaming about it. As a seventeen-year-old teenager, I was naïve, conservative, jealous and stupid, so I yelled at her for it and didn't talk to her for the last forty days of her life.

Saleema and I were very close. In my first year of primary school, her school was next to mine and we would go together. I remember when I was in Year Three; we were sitting in the garden when she told me an astonishing religious story about Joseph in the bible. She told me that his brother threw him into a well and then pretended that a fox ate him. I asked her where the story book was, so she gave it to me. It had about a thousand pages, which I read every summer.

The day she had the asthma attack, I came home in the afternoon and found her praying and reading the Quran. Looking at her, I knew she wasn't well but turned away and left without saying 'Hello'. My mother took her to hospital. At seven-thirty in the evening there was a knock at the door. A friend of my brother asked me to take my sister's ID to the hospital, telling me that she had passed away. Just like that. I couldn't believe it.

Saleema once told me that she wanted me to become a doctor so I could treat her asthma. She also told me about Iraq's tradition whereby the top ten students in Year Twelve would go on television. In the 80s, Saddam would even give the top ten students cars as a gift. She wanted me to be one of the top ten. She had tried herself but missed by a long way. A student had to get marks in the nineties to make it. Her dream was that I would be in the first ten, and become a doctor.

I was in shock. My brother's friend asked me why I was looking so terrible and to just take the ID to the hospital because there could be no death certificate without it. He said there was no room for emotion.

My mother told us that Saleema's asthma had become so serious that a doctor had given her an injection. Saleema then immediately turned blue and went into cardiac arrest. They couldn't revive her, and it was all happening in front of my mother – a terrible thing for her to have to watch. It was very hard for her. I believed that whatever they gave her caused the cardiac arrest. Now, as a doctor, I think they gave her aminophylline, the medication used in Iraq at the time for asthmatics. When the injection is given too quickly, it causes cardiac arrest. It is no longer used in Iraq.

By the time Saleema died, I was already acquainted with death and what it meant. With my father's death four years earlier I learnt that death was an end to all conversations.

What was unsaid remained unsaid. What was said could not be taken back.

And yet I still managed to alienate myself from Saleema in the forty days before her death. It was too late to fix it, ask for forgiveness, or get closure. I would never, ever have the opportunity to talk to her again.

I have a permanent hole in my heart over this. It will never heal. It's not a matter of guilt – I don't feel that about the situation now. Perhaps I did at the time. It's now all about closure, and that will never come to me.

I could say that at seventeen I couldn't possibly anticipate Saleema dying, but no one can anticipate death. I tell myself that a person is more stupid at that age, arrogant and stubborn.

I was upset with her, but that didn't mean I didn't love her. I also know in my heart that she would have soon forgiven me. I was a kid with a stupid kid's mouth. It was not about her death. We were accustomed to that in Iraq. Death is all around us. With Saleema, it's all about the things I have outstanding with her.

That's why I don't fight with anyone in the family anymore. Sometimes they don't talk to each other because of this or that, and I tell them that life is too short. We can lose the person we're arguing within the next second. I don't get upset with my brothers – whatever they say or do. It's not worth it.

I don't have words to describe how I much I cared for Saleema, but from time to time she comes to me in my dreams and I think that she's still alive. I wake up and realise I was dreaming.

The Emergency Force

In Year Eleven, when I was seventeen years old, I was walking in town with a cousin just before sunset. We stopped to talk to a friend when suddenly he ran away without a word. Turning around we saw what we thought were police. But, in fact, it was a highly trained para-military group called the Emergency Force.

They came up to us and started to hit our heads. We were then thrown into a big bus – it seemed most of the town's youth were already in there. Off we went to the police station where the Emergency Force men formed two lines into the station. Forcing us to walk through, we were beaten with fists and sticks. Behind bars, we asked each other what we'd done wrong. Absolutely nothing!

We weren't removed from our town, which meant that they weren't going to torture us. Ten of us were jammed in a cell two metres by two metres. With us all sitting on the floor, there wasn't a spare space left. It was dark, the only light coming in from outside.

I was beaten, receiving several stunning blows to my head, but I had committed no offence. It took a while to work out what was happening.

Apparently, a man who was 'absent without leave' from the army was being hunted. I was afraid that I'd be suspected of concealing information about his whereabouts, but I had no idea who or where he was.

After a couple of hours, my name was called and my ID checked. They asked if I was a student; I said that I was and they let me go. Outside I was released to Naeem and Hakeem who were waiting for me.

At least twice a month Saddam sent out his Emergency Force to the town to pick up any young men and put them in prison; it was one of the ways that Saddam created fear. If we had a legitimate reason for being out on the streets, like being a student or having finished army service, we were released. People frequently deserted from the army, which is one of the reasons Saddam sent the Emergency Force out.

My town was one of the three towns in Baghdad particularly targeted by the Emergency Force. The poorer areas and the south were targeted because they were generally dissatisfied with the government, whereas the rich areas remained untouched.

Aiming for top ten in Iraq

Two years after Saleema's death, I was in Year Twelve and decided to aim for top ten in Iraq and become a doctor. I'd worked hard at school but I would be competing against 50,000 Year Twelve students across the country, and my school had a poor reputation.

At the start of Year Twelve, my first lesson was physics. The teacher told us that if we wanted to do well in that year, we should cut all friendships and time-wasting activities – that included playing football. So that's what I did. I didn't go outside the house once I was home from school, and I put my friendships aside. School was from eight to one and then I studied for at least five hours each day. It became a routine and it proved to be the best advice I ever received.

From day one, I started to read all the textbooks. Many students bought the summaries but I couldn't afford them. The English teacher, Mr Wadda'ah, was a great person; he would come to school two hours early and take students from two classes for extra lessons in his own time. After school finished, he would take us again. He believed that repetition would make us better, and was very good with us.

He did have very high expectations. At first, Mr Wadda'ah underestimated my abilities. Then one day, he asked me to stand and read a passage. I did so, and then he asked me questions about it. It was very unusual for a student at our level to be able to read English well, but I answered him correctly. He told me that my English wasn't bad and to sit down. From then on, he kept an eye on me, always asking me questions.

After a while he realised that my English was in fact quite good and started to respect me a little. For example, if we came to those special classes later than six-thirty he usually wouldn't allow us in the room. I was late one day and he closed his eyes, pointed to my desk and told me to come in. That was unheard of.

One day Mr Wadda'ah smiled at me for the first time. English tests were done every couple of weeks and, studying so much, I was doing well in them. Then we had a mid-year exam which was both written and oral. I was the last out of 160 students to be orally tested and, when I went to see him, Mr Wadda'ah looked up, smiled and told me that I had full marks and didn't have to take it.

In the final Year Twelve English exams, I must have made a mistake somewhere because I scored ninety-nine. The next day, Mr Wadda'ah asked me what I got.

When I told him it was ninety-nine, he was so upset that he wouldn't talk to me and walked away. I understood, because winter and summer he'd been dedicating so much of his own time and he expected only the best. My brother studied under him a couple of years later and he told the class where I had made the mistake – I misspelled the name of one character in *The Merchant of Venice*!

Studying chemistry involved a lot of mathematics. Again, the teacher would give us tests every week and I always received full marks. I found a book that my uncle was using at university. It was in English and covered a lot of mathematical material, along with far more difficult questions than we had at school, so I started solving them. That helped me in the final Year Twelve exams because there was a question like the ones I studied in the book, and I was able to solve it.

A week later, my teacher found me at the markets and apologised for not teaching us the material that covered that question. Without mentioning the university book I'd been studying, I told him that it wasn't a problem as I'd worked it out. I got one hundred percent for the exam.

We'd been given forty days off to study before the final exams, so I went to my neighbour's place to have my hair cut to a 'zero' so I wouldn't go out. My family laughed at me but it made me stay home and study.

Later, they felt sorry for me because I became dizzy and collapsed the day before the maths exam. They asked me to take a break, so I went off and had an early night.

*

I knew I'd done well in the exams. We were given three hours for each exam and I finished chemistry in one hour, and maths in an hour and ten minutes. Saddam, deciding to become more religious, had just introduced a big curriculum of religious study and it was all new and difficult. I managed ninety-six for that. Arabic was a very tough exam and I managed ninety-one. Overall, I did well.

Life was difficult for everyone so there were no celebrations. We finished with school and got on with surviving.

I knew I'd done my best, but I didn't know how I would rank in the country's top ten. The exam results were due on a public holiday so the results weren't expected until the next day. I went off to work in a sewing thread factory in the Baghdad markets. Arriving home around two o'clock, I saw my brother sitting outside the house. He told me that the results were out and I'd got an average of 89. Not sure if he was joking or not, I went inside.

I was overwhelmed. My mother was making a *helahil*[1] whistling sound, she was so happy! It was the only time in her life that she did the *helahil*. It was an unbelievable time – not because my little sister told me that my average was 97.6 – but because it was the only time I saw my mother happy. The sound of my mother's happiness still echoes in my ears. I am proud that I had made her happy, took her out of that endless sadness, even for a short time.

And, I did it all for my sister, Saleema. I wish I'd been a doctor before her death, because I now know that I could have treated her and she wouldn't have died. I never want to see patients die when it can be prevented. I take that very seriously.

A few years later, as a doctor in emergency, a lady of Saleema's age came in with her mother. She had very bad asthma and I became fixated about saving her. I initiated treatment and then contacted one of the intensive care doctors to help me. I was so relieved when she started to recover and began talking.

In my life, there are two achievements I'm most happy about. The first is that I made top ten in Iraq: the previous time anyone in my small school made the top ten was in 1961. The second is that I became a doctor.

Saleema wanted me to do both those things.

---

1. Arab women make a sound or ululation, a long, wavering, high-pitched, trilling sound made to honour someone and made at a time of extreme happiness.

Naeem and the police

The day my Year Twelve exam results came out, my brother Naeem was in trouble. He was arrested and imprisoned. Everyone in our town knew that one son of my deceased father was going to prison and the other had received the highest mark in town. The town didn't consider my mother to be a bad mum, unable to raise her children properly because, for them, the good news of my achievement overshadowed the bad. More so, when the next day, I was ranked number eight in the whole of Iraq.

But how did Naeem end up getting into trouble?

In the school year of 1990–1991, my brother Naeem, older than me by two years, was with me in Year Eight. He'd failed in his second year of primary school, and again in Year Six. The school didn't really care that they failed him twice, and his disruptive nature was disliked by the teachers.

Naeem was a good person but he didn't study, and he'd hang around with the naughty boys. I tried to help him before each exam, teaching him each subject. Although he passed most subjects, he still failed in two and dropped out of school to join the police rather than the army.

They gave him a salary of three or four dollars per month. Corruption crept into the police because three dollars was not enough to buy even one shirt. It was the same in the army as well. The policy of the government was to offer low salaries so that it would attract people who were morally corrupt, which seemed to help the government stay in power. The entire police force was corrupt, including the Minister of Police who was Saddam's brother.

Sadly, the corruption in the police suited Naeem's personality. Charged with misbehaving and failing to do his duty, he was imprisoned for the first time. I was told that he took a bribe and was caught, but I can't be sure.

He spent eight days in prison; we got him out by paying US$1,500. His case was cancelled and he resumed his police duties. Admittedly, he was doing the wrong thing, but he was only put in prison in order to extract money – that's how things were done.

If you were smart, you tried to avoid those possibilities by not working for the government.

University

In Iraq, all universities are free. Undergraduate students apply with a list of their university preferences and the students are placed according to their marks. There are thirteen medical schools in Iraq and scoring ninety-seven or above entitled me to attend the medical school in Baghdad. Actually, with my mark I could have chosen any medical school.

One of my close friends from high school was called Salim Al-Yaqoubi. He had gone on to study nursing and when I finished high school, Salim contacted me to say that the Saddam University had an excellent medical school and it was reasonably close to my town.

Usually students applied with their preferences and the Minister of Education would allocate them according to their mark. With Saddam University, students had to apply directly. The university would then assess them with tests and an interview. Until then, I'd never heard of Saddam University but was told that it was challenging and that the university also provided a wage for its students.

On applying, I was told that I should sit the test. My friends didn't like the idea because the university was directly linked to Saddam Hussein. It was also linked to Uday Hussein, Saddam's son, who was notorious for torturing people. However, the difficulty of entry appealed to me and they *did* pay a wage. Accepting only fifty students a year, they combined the average from the high school marks with the results of their test to make a decision.

There were about a thousand applicants from all over Iraq and the exam consisted of twenty pages, all in English. Physics, chemistry, biology and English language were in that one test. It was extremely difficult and, when I'd finished, I thought that perhaps I'd got half of the answers right. A few days later, I was informed that I'd come seventeenth and had been accepted. Later, I discovered that there was only one high school in Iraq that studied in English. Twelve of the students accepted were from that school and passed the exam easily. But, I was in!

My oldest brother, Saleem, told me in Year Twelve that if I got into medical school he would give me a thousand Iraqi dinars. He never gave me the money. Maybe now I should ask him for it.

*

On the first day of university, I arrived at eight-thirty expecting to start at nine but couldn't find anyone. Thinking I should go home, I was about to leave when the guard asked if I was new, and then pointed me in the direction of a lady from administration who informed me that I was late and that the classes started at eight. She took me to a classroom where the students were studying computer science.

I'd never owned or even used a computer before, and here I was with the top students of Iraq, who all came from wealthy families. Most of them had owned computers and used them for years. Intelligent and nerdy, they represented a very new world to me.

I had no idea what the lecturer was talking about and I could see that everyone was smart. Completely different to my old school mates, these students were intense, serious, didn't laugh or make jokes, and lacked basic social skills. The person behind me was behaving oddly, so I mentioned it to a student sitting nearby. 'Don't talk about our colleagues like that,' he told me. *Right. Got it*, I thought.

Regardless of my ignorance, I was keen to learn and ended up getting good marks. It took a while to settle in to all the subjects because all the lectures were in English and, not having done any listening of the language in high school, I struggled for the first four months. Although my hearing of English was improving, I read the textbooks rather than my lecture notes and managed to keep up. It was a hard year, yet I managed to come in fifth out of fifty.

In the first year, I began to get to know people and make friends. We had a good mix; most students were from Baghdad, quite a few were from the other provinces, and three were Kurds. When Saddam decided that the Kurds were to be expelled it upset us all. By that time, we'd all become friends. However, the Kurdish students were happy. Transferred to the four hundred-student Baghdad University, they found the social life better and, with the fifty percent pass mark requirement, the pressure less intense. Our pass mark was sixty-five percent, and if we missed three lectures we were expelled.

There were about seventeen girls in the course and none of us had much in the way of social skills. As a result, we boys split into two groups – good guys and bad guys. The girls wouldn't talk to us 'bad boys'. The division sometimes caused fights and created tensions among us.

We, the bad guys, were relaxed, going to parties and having fun. The so-called 'good guys' pretended to study to impress the ladies and stayed away from the fun times. In those days, we were free to mix with girls but I doubt that it's the same these days.

My monthly pay from university was 300 dinars. That was a lot of money when the university was founded seven years earlier, however, by the time I was there, inflation meant that 300 dinars could buy just four burgers. Things had to change.

*

At the end of my first year, I had to find a job. Dhafir, one of my high school friends, asked me to join him in his shop, buying packets of cigarettes and selling them individually. Dhafir had no idea what his profit or loss was because he had no bookwork – in fact, he'd been losing money, probably through a dishonest helper he'd let go. The first thing I did was buy a notebook and write down his inventory, then what he bought and sold. We soon had a pretty good idea of what was working, made a few changes and moved his business into profit.

I was no stranger to selling things.

In Year Three, my brother, Hakeem, was selling vegetables in the town's main street. One day he asked me why I wasn't helping him – I started relieving him for a few hours each day so he could have a break. I did that all the summer without being paid. Hakeem didn't pay me because he used the money to buy food for the household, and he believed that I should be helping the family too.

Now, after buying the cigarettes at the big market, I worked in Dhafir's shop from seven to eleven in the evenings. It was enjoyable work and at the end of each day, I'd calculate how much we'd earned and split the profit. I wanted to continue but in my second year of university, I found that my academic ranking had dropped from five to twenty-seven. I was really disappointed and told Dhafir reluctantly that I had to quit. The job had badly affected my studies and putting that right was a priority.

Uday Hussein

Uday Hussein was the head of the Iraqi Olympic Committee, the head of the Iraqi Football Federation, and was responsible for the Saddam Hussein University. He also put together a cruel and merciless militia group called Fidayeen Saddam, who would sacrifice their lives for Saddam. They committed many crimes and would torture people until they got the information they wanted. Uday made this group's activities public because he wanted to spread fear of him. Saddam's other son, Quday, ran the Presidential Guard.

After the exams at the end of the first semester in 1996, we had ten days off. A couple of friends and I went off to a very wealthy area in Baghdad called Al-Mansor, where people could walk around the nice shops and have an ice cream.

Near the ice cream shop, we suddenly heard gunshots. Spinning around, we saw a bullet shatter the windscreen of a car. Everyone escaped into the shops and waited fearfully. The gunfire stopped for about twenty seconds and then started again. Running to another part of the town we heard people saying that Uday had been shot.

Returning to the area of the gunfire shortly afterwards, we saw Uday's car across the street and Adidas bags on the ground. It appeared that the people who'd attacked him had been carrying the weapons in them. We realised that if Uday had been shot, we could be caught up in the investigation, so we decided to leave quickly.

In the taxi home, we saw that the Emergency Forces had blocked off the whole area. We were lucky to escape. The next night it was announced on the evening news that Uday had been shot. That night, our entire town knew that my friends and I had been there and we became heroes. It was almost like we'd shot him ourselves. My two friends and I were asked to tell our story but, after a while, thought it best to go home and stay there. The last thing we wanted was to be questioned by the authorities because, innocent or guilty, that always ended badly.

Uday had been shot in his car and hit by fourteen bullets. He survived the attack but was paralysed. People celebrated. It was widely known that he raped women. Paralysis meant that his penis was out of action.

Military training

In 1998, my fourth year at medical school, Saddam called for all Iraqi to volunteer for military training. The head of our university said that because our university carried the name of Saddam, everyone had to volunteer.

Military training

At midday the next day, lessons were stopped and all the university students, lecturers, professors and employees changed into military uniforms and spent the next two hours training.

The instructors were tough, uneducated military men and they were harsh. They imposed full army training procedures, including punishments. We complained and, luckily, the professors all seemed to have had the same horrible experience. The Dean intervened, requesting more educated officers, and on the second day, decent people (who were also graduates) arrived.

We were taught how to use weapons, including the AK-47. We were shown how to dismantle it and put it back together. That wasn't hard as it is quite a simple weapon. Then, it was off to the firing range. I loathed that and didn't want to fire the thing. Luckily, it was extremely disorganised there, so nobody saw me fail to fire it. Other friends didn't use it either. The weapons were designed to kill and as trainee doctors, that's not what we were about. We were all peaceful people. However, we did enjoy each other's company during the training. It got us out of lectures and was a bit of fun.

On 18 April 1998, we paraded in front of Saddam Hussein. When we passed him, we had to turn our heads in his direction. We were meant to turn our heads back to face front, but I continued to stare at him. I wanted to get a good look at the man that caused us so much trouble.

This photo was taken in April 1998 in the medical school's gardens while doing military training. I am the first from the left, seated.

Elections in Iraq

Back in 1995 when I was my second year, Saddam Hussein declared a public holiday so an election could be held. The election question was, 'Do you want Saddam Hussein to be the President of Iraq. Yes or No?' Older than eighteen, I had the right to vote so I went to the school, found my name and picked up my voting paper from a Ba'ath Party man who told me to vote 'yes'. That annoyed me so I told him that I could vote 'yes' or 'no'. I then put 'no' on the paper and held it up so the overseeing judges could see and then dropped it in the ballot box. It was a very, very stupid thing to do.

Two weeks later, my brothers Naeem and Saleem asked me if I had really voted 'no'. They were angry and questioned me about the incident, telling me that I was dumb and that the government had taken two families from our town and killed them because they had voted 'no'. Fortunately, they didn't come to get us. I believe they hadn't recognised me because I hadn't been around the area for a couple of years, spending all my time at university.

When the election results were published, it was declared that one hundred percent of the votes were 'yes'. My mother spoke out. She knew that one of her sons had voted 'no'.

But my family wouldn't allow me to vote in the second election in 2002.

Finishing University

In 2000, after six years of study, I finished medical school. I was excited because it had been very tough and now all the hard work and study had paid off. I had friends from both a higher socio-economic group and different parts of Baghdad. I now knew of, and was part of, a different world.

The entire time, I'd held onto my dream of becoming a doctor and here I was.

In medical school I made friendships that became important to my life. Because the university was related to Saddam, the lecturers pushed us harder than anywhere else in Iraq: three exams a day meant constant study. The pressure forged strong bonds between people from different religious backgrounds, different characteristics and wildly different socio-economic backgrounds. We formed a group of twelve friends.

Firas was a big man who did body building. His father was a professor and the family had gone to the United Kingdom when he was a baby. They moved back to Iraq but Firas always dreamed of returning to the UK one day. They were well off and lived in a wealthy area. I would spend a great deal of time there. Firas, like many of my friends, was very smart. But Firas was extremely lazy and wouldn't take notes in lectures, he'd just sit and chat whereas I had to listen and take notes or fail.

Yet Firas never failed. He was so bright that one day before the exams, he'd come to my house and we'd go through the lectures. His eyes would blink rapidly as I carefully explained everything to him and he'd have it all in one day. Amazing intelligence. He told me that he admired me for coming from a poor area and showing strength and courage. He believed that I had a lot to offer.

On the first day of university I met Ali Amir – handsome, white-skinned and long-haired – who, through his charisma and popularity, became the group's leader. He sat beside me that day and asked if we could become friends.

In my second year, Ali asked me to join his group of friends from the same high school. Being friends with everyone, I wasn't aware there was such a group.

The focus of the group was enjoyment, fun and maintaining decent morals. For example, talking about people behind their backs was frowned upon and it was my stance on that issue that got me into the group.

We developed notoriety in the college for causing trouble. We'd come into the cafeteria laughing loudly and being disruptive, and everyone else would leave. At our graduation party, we went a bit wild, with the rest of the school happy to just watch on. We were a little crazy and swore that we'd stay together.

After the war, we began to go our separate ways. As each of us left, it was an emotional time and I was saddened by it. Now, there are three of us in America, two in Canada, three in the UK, one in Dubai, one in Malaysia and me in Australia.

We're all well-behaved consultants now.

Seven of us have remained in contact. Through a difficult time in Iraq, we supported and helped each other with our studies. When we entered the hospital system, we worked at the same hospital and continued that support.

Looking back, the five who went their own way clearly felt differently about friendship, morals and loyalty. There was a lot of discussion about friendships back then and the five who lost contact weren't interested in being part of them.

Celebrations

Two celebrations marked the end of medical school, one in the morning and another in the evening. The morning one wasn't much. The two groups that made up the school had photos taken with the head of school and that was basically it. The evening function was held in the university gardens – we'd worked for two days making the gardens look good. We bought some expensive disco lights and, to pay for them, we charged everyone who attended a one-dollar fee.

Finding the entry fee for my family was tough. Luckily, I'd won first prize for some research I'd submitted for a conference the week before. It was five dollars which meant that Mum, Saleem and Naeem could attend.

There was no alcohol at the celebrations because it was a family event. I have never had alcohol and if anyone drank it in Iraq, it was done privately. Muslims do not drink alcohol and there's social stigma attached to drinking. Our university also had no drug issues because in Saddam's time, drug-use resulted in execution. The law was strict – touch drugs, smell them, sell them and it was the death penalty. It is very different in Iraq now: drugs have become a real problem.

My friends and I did not need alcohol to be drunk. The party officially finished at two o'clock in the morning, but we stayed until morning. We were so full of energy and laughing hysterically, not because we had graduated but because it was a party. Relieved of the enormous pressure of study, and being young, we danced like monkeys for hours.

The other students enjoyed our madness but wouldn't join in. However, they told us that they were inspired by our spontaneous behaviour, our generosity and love, the help we extended to younger students, and our moral strength. I recall one student who failed third year. We tried to help him but he buckled under the pressure. Heading off to another university in Baghdad, he found his niche and ranked nine out of five hundred. He's now a dermatologist in Iraq.

Graduation, September 2001. I am second from the left, standing.

Working at the hospital

For some years during university, we'd been going to the hospital connected to the medical school for practical lessons. Ours was attached to the President while other hospitals were attached to the Ministry of Health. Our salary was much better, working at the Presidential hospital. At the Ministry of Health hospitals, new doctors were paid five to six dollars per month. At fifty to sixty dollars per month, we were much better off. I could live on that. I could buy food and clothes but I couldn't save.

One day I visited another hospital and met a man working there who was very bright. He'd been ranked third at his university and was working fifteen on-calls (twenty-four-hour shifts) per month. With a salary of 11,000 Iraqi dinars – about six or seven dollars – he still needed his parents' money to survive. He had only one old, low-quality shirt and as he was from another province, he couldn't afford to visit his parents at all. I told him if I'd been in his position I would have given up, and asked him why he was doing it. 'I'm just trying to build up a good reputation,' he told me, 'because I hope something will happen for me in the future.'

I was lucky. Our university took in only fifty student doctors every year and only those students went to the attached hospital. With twelve hundred graduating doctors each year in Iraq, the doctors in the Ministry of Health hospitals suffered terrible pay and couldn't afford anything. However, the social position and community respect were good.

Two weeks before I started my first shift at the hospital, we had to repeat the Hippocratic Oath because it had changed. The new version started with 'I swear by God I will support the revolution of 17 July, I support Saddam Hussein and I will protect Iraq.' All about Saddam, not about the patient. The Head of School started speaking the oath for us to repeat after him, but I only moved my mouth and a lot of my friends did the same. I was not going to swear by God that I would support the revolution and Saddam's government. For me, it was most important that I not do so.

Seven months after starting at the hospital we had still not been paid our salary. The authorities were checking on us; our parents, our grandparents and great-grandparents to ensure we didn't have family roots in Iran. If there were any links to that country, we couldn't work at that hospital. The process took seven months and we weren't paid until every graduate was checked. We had no warning, and this was the first time it had happened – the graduates from the previous year had been paid quite quickly.

Starting in the tough area of internal medicine, I was on-call for twenty-four hours on my first day. A friend, Mahmood, stayed to support me, something we'd decided to do for each other. The night was busy and difficult with constant resuscitations and CPR but I pulled through it.

Two patients died overnight – something quite common back then. Iraqi doctors are trained to be resilient to death. It's not that we lack emotion or that we don't feel empathetic – far from it. It's more like compartmentalisation. We are doing one task, something very focused and if there is a death, then we put it into a little box. That way we keep an empathetic demeanour towards our patients' families but maintain strength for them to draw on. And then we're likely to go back into the battle minutes later and do it all again.

I liked internal medicine, a combination of cardiology, respiratory medicine and all the conditions treated by medical care rather than surgery. In Australia, it's known as general medicine.

My friend Mahmood was one of the twelve friends from university; he was with me on all the rotations. He is so close to me that we think of ourselves as twins. He comes from a big family and has two other brothers who are doctors, two brothers who are engineers, and a sister who is a civil engineer. He certainly comes from an intelligent and educated family.

His father is also a highly educated man, and a high-ranking army officer. I would sit and listen to his wisdom for hours. Mahmood's mother was like my second mother and I would kiss her on top of her head, something a person only does to his mother. In fact, I used to call her 'Mum'.

Mahmood also grew up in a poor area so we had a lot in common. He is Sunnite, but this never affected our relationship. He's very funny and his sense of humour has everyone rolling with laughter as soon as he opens his mouth. A real comedian.

A very caring person, he is obsessed with all patients' welfare. On his first on-call, he was attending one of the patients who needed a blood transfusion. He was so caring he was measuring the patient's blood pressure every fifteen minutes. We usually cared for at least eighty patients during an on-call shift and couldn't possibly give the same care to everyone as Mahmood was giving.

Mahmood admitted that he couldn't do on-call his way but couldn't accept doing it any differently. So, he made the decision to choose a non-clinical path. But Mahmood needed to complete his one year of clinical internship before he could go on to study for his masters. That was a problem.

That year, he still needed to do six twenty-four hour on-calls a month for three months. So, Mahmood went to the hospital in the morning, did the rounds with the consultant and performed the morning's work, and then paid me to do his on-calls. After that year, he went on to do a master's degree in microbiology, and is now involved in teaching and lab work, away from the patients.

Helping Mahmood helped me in two ways: I started to get good money, and all the double shifts exposed me to a huge variety of medical conditions. Arduous and difficult though it was, I did revel in the great training it afforded me. Later, I also took Mahmood's emergency department and paediatric on-calls. Apart from all that, I put my hand up for extra paid shifts, so I was able to survive in the first seven months with some money.

Very soon after Mahmood and I began our rotations, we had a patient with advanced lymphoma and sepsis. He was very old, had been unconscious for two days with low blood pressure and multi-organ failure. His prognosis was very poor. We started him on medication to raise his blood pressure.

In Australia, in similar situations, we do not follow the same approach. With a cardiac arrest, we don't resuscitate the patient as it's a futile exercise. In all other cases, after discussion with the patient's family, we set the limitations of treatment. We will suggest a palliative care approach as the most appropriate medical intervention, an approach I believe provides more dignity to the patient.

In Iraq, sadly, we have to resuscitate every single patient despite the obvious futility of such intervention. In addition to that, the resuscitations are usually done by very inexperienced junior doctors, mostly interns, compared with Australia where we have emergency teams consisting of very experienced senior doctors and nurses attending what we call 'Code Blue'.

When the nurse called me, Mahmood and I attended the patient and realised that the very old patient wasn't breathing. We did CPR with his family in attendance. We gave him breathing support and shocked him three times. After forty minutes, we checked his eye responses, his cardiac rhythm, his breathing, and I pronounced him dead. I wasn't affected at the time and managed the procedures without any problem. But I was glad to have

Mahmood with me. It was the start, and I was confronted with another death later that night.

No medicines, just corruption

What I disliked most about the work was the lack of medicine. As the only doctor in the emergency department at night, I'd be told by the pharmacist what medications he had. That would be five ampoules of Voltarin for pain, five Valium for anxiety and five Lasix to treat fluid retention. I had to manage every patient who came into emergency with that and no more.

It was Saddam's policy to make the people suffer by not providing adequate medical supplies to hospitals. Saddam could then declare that the United Nations sanctions on Iraq were causing people to die. After the war, tonnes and tonnes of medical supplies were found stored in a warehouse.

At night-time people came in with treatable diseases, so it was frustrating that medicine was kept from us. But the hospital management was also corrupt. Dr Hakam was the head of the hospital administration. Initially, hospital care was a free service. He made patients pay. For example, a teacher's pay was three to four thousand dinars a month and he charged 25,000 dinar for hospital admission. And he would charge the patient for any of the limited medicine we could give them.

The profit from this was meant to be distributed amongst the doctors and staff at the hospital but management grabbed it. An MRI cost four million Iraqi dinars – about US$40,000 – and that went to the radiologist. I would work very hard: fifteen shifts of twenty-four hours each month in dialysis or the paediatric unit and receive 600 Iraqi dinars – less than one US dollar. It was very unfair.

Patients paid for treatment: doctors and nursing staff got nothing. The fees went to management – the director of the hospital and the people working in administration. One man in the finance department designed the system so the finance department received two or three million dinars a month. They were like a cartel, manipulating the system to get rich.

Corruption was everywhere in the hospital. The director, believed to be one of Saddam's relatives, was a political appointee. Before the war, he used Saddam's family name to make people afraid of him, but afterwards changed his name. The doctors who were the heads of departments supported the government and were vindictive. Harsh on my friends and me, they found fault at every turn and would punish us.

The senior staff treated us like slaves. For example, a doctor in paediatrics would bully all of us, and we couldn't say anything because he was Ba'ath Party and part of the regime. Although we tried to reason with him, he'd wait until seven-thirty when we'd gone for dinner, go to the ward and announce that he was unable to find a doctor there. That would mean a cut in salary of ten percent.

I was diplomatic, worked hard and tried not to make mistakes so I was never punished, but some my friends would do stupid things and get punished, along with some good guys who were inadvertently involved. It was leadership by bullying, and an unhealthy environment where the senior staff failed to communicate with interns. We were better off at night on-call when we were left to our own devices and could meet colleagues working in other departments. When not on-call, we would stay in the hospital accommodation.

Naeem finds trouble

For some time while I was at medical school, Naeem had been working as a guard in police storage. In 2000, he and some friends stole some redundant spare parts and sold them. He was arrested at work in early December, just a week after the birth of his son. We couldn't see him for three weeks. He called once and told me that all his nails had been pulled out, he'd been badly beaten and tortured repeatedly, and blood was appearing in his urine. As a doctor, I knew that meant kidney damage. He was crying, in severe pain, couldn't go on talking, and then the line dropped out.

When we saw Naeem for the first time after his arrest, he was dreadfully pale and held me tightly and kissed me before showing me the bones that had been broken in his arms. To my horror, he'd received no medical treatment for the fractures and the bones had been left to heal by themselves.

In the prison where he was held, visits were permitted for only ten minutes every fortnight (one week for male visitors and the other for female visitors). Each time, with at least 1,500 visitors wanting to see their loved ones, we would queue for hours before being allowed into the cells with forty other visitors.

We could hardly see Naeem. Sometimes, if we were lucky, we could touch his hand through the bars. I never skipped a visit. Hakeem, Ahmed and Mohammed would go from the house and I would go from the hospital. I would give Naeem money – whatever I had – as he needed it for everything, even having a bath or watching TV. Everything required money.

He was in prison for ten months. Life stood still for the family. We didn't talk about him, nobody smiled and everyone prayed to God. We stayed at our home as our relatives visited.

His trial was set for 1 July.

When we heard that date, my brothers Saleem and Hakeem tried to find a way to help Naeem. Unfortunately, the first investigation and interrogation reports confirmed that Naeem and two of his friends had confessed. My brother said he knew about a lawyer who was very high in the police and part of Saddam's regime. The lawyer knew the judge and my brothers thought he might help us. I went with my two brothers to see the lawyer who requested a very large sum of money – around five million Iraqi dinars, something impossible for us to get.

I had now been working as a doctor for seven months so I had just received all the pay owed to me. It was good money. Telling my friends about the situation with Naeem and what I had in the way of money, they went by car to every friend's home and collected cash. They collected three and a half million Iraqi dinar and delivered it to me. We made a deal with the lawyer that if he succeeded, great – but if he didn't, he would keep one-and-a-half million and give three-and-a-half back. We paid him, but on the first day of the trial in July, the court wouldn't allow the lawyer to enter the courtroom.

The police had put Naeem before a special Presidential Court where there was a judge, but lawyers weren't permitted. There were no appeals: the decisions of that court were final.

It wasn't a real trial: Naeem wasn't allowed to defend himself, and his lawyer wasn't allowed into the court. It was a court by name only as Saddam had already decided the outcome.

After ten minutes, the judge decided that it would be execution in forty-five days.

In that short space of time, Naeem and three of his friends were tried and condemned to death. Naeem told us this after the hearing because we hadn't been allowed anywhere near the courtroom.

Naeem had confessed under torture and the court accepted the preliminary investigation from that questioning, despite it being extracted under extreme pain. I don't know why his case was taken to the Presidential Court but it was extremely bad luck. It was the court for political prisoners – and theft wasn't political.

Waiting for execution

All of us, apart from Saleem and Hakeem, had waited at home on the day of Naeem's trial. Hakeem saw the lawyer, who said that he hadn't been allowed inside the courtroom – and that Naeem would be executed.

When Saleem and Hakeem came back to us at home, they were weeping. We were shocked. That was a very hard day for us all.

Two days later, we could visit Naeem in prison but none of the family wanted to go. Hakeem and Saleem said that they didn't know what to say to him. I decided to go and a cousin came with me. The first thing Naeem said was that I was loyal to Saddam. I don't know where he got the idea but I didn't argue.

I knew deep in myself that I had very strong view against Saddam and his regime and about the injustice that had developed over the years. All my life I've been thoughtful about my actions, always guided by my principles, choosing what is correct, and what is wrong. My ideology had developed from an early age and Naeem's trial was just a confirmation of the unfairness that the regime represented.

The days passed and we couldn't do anything.

Saleem was a lecturer at university where one of his students was the son of the vice-president of Iraq. The student really liked Saleem because he was a good lecturer and at times Saleem had given him private tutorials. Saleem told the student about Naeem; the student passed it on to his father. We were hoping for a pardon or something that would help. A few days later, Saddam was on TV, declaring that it was no use sending representation for a pardon because the government wouldn't pardon criminals. He was referring to Naeem. It was a shock and we knew that things were bad.

Waiting for execution

In Iraq, 8 August 1998 was an important date commemorating the end of the war between Iran and Iraq. Even though Saddam had lost the war, he regarded it as a day of great victory and celebrated it every year. We thought Saddam would pardon some prisoners on 8 August 2001. When we visited Naeem on the fifteenth we asked if anything like that had happened and he told us that Saddam had decided to celebrate the day: with the execution of eighty-eight people.

Naeem would be one of them.

Of my family, all but Saleem went to visit him. I don't know why Saleem didn't go to say goodbye. When we arrived at the prison, there were thousands of people who'd arrived to see the prisoners. We could tell from their clothes that they were all from the south and mostly Shi'a.

August 29th was to be Naeem's last day.

It was a very, very bad day.

*

The loss of a loved one is a terrible thing. The grief is crushing, bleak, with no end in sight. When death is mixed with injustice, there's a special taste of bitterness added to the sorrow.

In the final days I went with Naeem's wife and children to visit him in prison. Our mother hadn't arrived to join us by the time we were to go in and we were unable to wait. Entering a door to find eight cells on either side of a corridor, we saw that Naeem and all the prisoners for execution were in a single cell. Each cell had a tiny window and that was the only way a visitor could talk to the condemned – through that small, impersonal gap.

All around there were people shouting and weeping. When we found my brother, he hadn't realised that we had arrived. He was quiet and leaning forward in prayer.

When Naeem finished praying, he raised his head and saw us. He smiled, giving that awful visit some meaning for us all. He was brave and talked easily, glad to see his wife and three children, but deeply concerned about our mother.

Then she arrived.

As she walked towards Naeem's cell, he raised his hand to stop her. It was too distressing for him. At that moment, he broke down and wept.

'I'm so sorry,' he told our mother. 'I've given you a hard time for all my life. Please forgive me.'

Naeem faced his end with only consideration for others, assuring us that we shouldn't be distressed for him because he was going to God. 'God is kind,' he told us. 'But Saddam is not. I feel for you who will suffer badly under him.'

We had an hour with him. In past prison visits, I had given Naeem money. This time he handed me all his money, and told me that he no longer needed it. 'I'll keep my watch for now,' he said. 'When it's my time I'll give it to our neighbour who works here. He will bring it to you and when you receive it, you'll know that I'm dead. Please keep it for my older boy and give it to him when he grows up.'

With great sorrow, we left.

Our mother was missing again. We returned to find her at the back of a room where a small window allowed her to see Naeem.

She simply could not leave him.

After my brother's execution, a veil of deep sadness fell on our home. A song

My late brother, Naeem.

My mother and brother Hakeem, visiting the tomb of Naeem.

would come on TV and everyone would cry. One song that really touched us was *I Love You, By God I Love You*, about separation from family, travelling, and how much the singer loved and missed his family. There was also an Egyptian drama that we were watching on television where one of the characters was sent to prison because of an injustice. Reminded of Naeem, my family started crying.

The grief remained for a long time but we didn't really talk about it. In Iraq, our way was to turn to God. Everyone started to pray, which gave us some comfort. We also visited his grave every year. The *Hajj* is the annual Islamic pilgrimage to Mecca, after which we celebrate *Eid al-Adha*. In the first day of *Eid al-Adha*, families – millions of us – visit the graves of our ancestors. On the second day, we visit our relatives and celebrate with them.

Another execution?

Two people from the local council in our town had been complicit in getting Naeem in trouble. They had taken a lot of money from us saying they'd help him in his case but did nothing. They were using our vulnerability to get money from us and, in fact, made things unpleasant for him in prison through their police contacts.

A week before Naeem's execution, they came to our house to talk to Hakeem, who was liaising with them and had given them a lot of money in the hope they could help us find a way out for Naeem.

I was working at the hospital the day they came to our home. My family told me that they were very angry when they saw them laughing at the door, especially as Naeem was about to be executed. Hakeem, all my other younger brothers and sister, Naeem's wife and my mother started throwing shoes and stones at them, and chased them away.

It just so happened that someone arrived from the prison at the same time with a notification that Naeem would be executed the following week. Hakeem angrily tore it up. What nobody knew at the time was that it wasn't an official notification but a note from a friend working in the prison giving us warning that Naeem's execution date had been set.

The official notification came only one day before the execution.

After Naeem's execution, the two men who'd been chased away reported Hakeem to the government, stating that Hakeem insulted them and shouted bad things about Saddam Hussein and the revolution. It was outright lies. All Hakeem had shouted was the fact that they'd got Naeem imprisoned, taken money from us, and then come to our house laughing. They put in their report that Hakeem had destroyed the official notification that was sent to the family. That report went to the local council and government party.

It was the sort of accusation that guaranteed Hakeem's execution.

Exactly one month after Naeem's execution, we received notification that Hakeem was to surrender himself to the local government party to investigate his insulting the revolution. We thought about sending Hakeem to the south to escape from Baghdad, but we knew that would result in our house being destroyed and our entire family taken away. Aware that anyone accused of insulting the government faced certain death, we were desperately afraid and couldn't figure out what to do.

That morning, Hakeem was very brave. He went to the investigators, taking the official notification we'd received the day before Naeem's execution. The investigators showed Hakeem the report and asked him to respond. Hakeem told them how the two guys initially came to our house, telling us that they would help get Naeem out of prison. Hakeem also told them that the men had asked to be paid in American dollars, to which Hakeem had replied, 'To be honest, I have never seen American dollars before, and I struggled to get them. I gave them Iraqi dinars instead.'

He told them about the two men coming back to the house and laughing out the front. He admitted that the family were in a very emotional state and had chased the guys off, but had never insulted the government. When the investigators asked him about the crime of tearing up the official notification, Hakeem produced it and said that it proved that he was telling the truth. That notification ruined the two men's credibility and saved Hakeem's life. The investigators told Hakeem not to worry and that he could leave. Of course, the two men were never punished.

I am very patient. If I'd been at the house at the time, I would have ignored the guys laughing and encouraged everyone to stay calm. Instead, the whole family lost it and because the two men had been humiliated in front of a crowd, they took revenge.

That was such a difficult time for us in 2001: Naeem's execution and the possibility of losing another brother just a month later. And in between, came 9/11.

9/11

My rotation as an intern had just started when Naeem was executed. I couldn't tell the hospital, but my friends who did know told me to go home and they would look after all my on-calls.

I wondered if I'd be kicked out of medicine because of Naeem. At the time, I was working as a registrar – a senior position – as part of my training. But I needn't have worried: cataclysmic world events were about to unfold and my reputation would be insignificant.

Just back at work, I was going to the doctors' accommodation when I saw forty-odd doctors standing around the TV. I could see aeroplanes hitting buildings. I remember it was horrific but there seemed to be a lot of happiness in the room at the same time. Grieving, I couldn't relate to it and walked on.

Leaving them, I went to Mahmood's room. He told me that he had spoken to his father, ranked very highly in the Iraqi army, who was very worried. He had said that what had happened in America would cause trouble. Mahmood was frightened and agitated, and the only person who looked at those events with caution. That stuck in my mind and, thinking back, Mahmood's father was a very wise person. He predicted what would happen – a disaster.

The war ten years before had been hard on us. During Desert Storm, the US destroyed the water supply, electricity was not available for two months, and then it was three hours on and three hours off. There was no food. There was no medicine and people were dying. People ate food that was meant for animals. The US destroyed the infrastructure of Iraq and everyone blamed America. Instead of getting rid of Saddam, they destroyed all of Iraq. Both Saddam and America were blamed. The Americans didn't think that people were dying, but innocent people *were*.

In the media, we only had one channel, run politically by Saddam. As a result, the TV always blamed America for Desert Storm, but Saddam's stupidity caused it.

The people who died in the 9/11 incidents were also innocent. They had no relationship to the government or the people making the decisions, or the people who would benefit from the war, like the weapons manufacturers and the oil producers.

It was a mess and we would suffer again because of it.

Part Two:
The Hospital

Hospital life

As an intern, I deeply cared for my patients and worked long, hard hours to help them as much as possible under the most difficult circumstances. But we were poorly trained and under enormous pressure. In emergency, I'd see hundreds of patients each day as they lined up for hours, whereas in Australia the training is different and doctors take care of eight patients over eight hours.

Some patients would come to the hospital with mental health issues, others with physical problems. Mental health issues were referred to as 'histrionics'. People would come in stressed, complaining of chest pains. We could diagnose them but were then managing them incorrectly. We were inflicting pain on these patients. It was what we were trained to do.

I remember a seventeen-year-old girl whose family was upset because she was paralysed; her legs were not moving and she was unable to walk. I examined her and clearly it was psychological. I asked the family to wait outside and gave her Lasix, which was the only medication I had. It would make her pee. Then I told the parents that she would be walking in ten to fifteen minutes. In fact, she ran to the toilet and I heard her family happily chanting their prayers. In Australia, I'd be deregistered for doing something like that. Of course, I feel ashamed now but that was how we were trained.

If patients came in screaming with a psychosomatic ailment, we'd have ten family members with them, shouting as well. We found that patients, trying to get attention, would present with very weird symptoms that frightened the rest of the family. Telling the family that the problem was psychological would create an enormous fuss, and the family would disagree. Often doctors were punched by the patient's relatives.

We had no training for treating psychological problems, so, what did we do? We gave the patient one milligram of aminophylline administered intramuscularly. When given that way, the medication causes terrible pain. The injection had no damaging effect on the patient, it just inflicted pain. With chest pain, the patient would immediately stop shouting. They'd also get a sore bottom. Then they'd leave. That was terrible training. We just didn't know how to treat people with psychological problems.

In other areas, we were doing a great job despite working under great difficulty. Our main stumbling blocks were a lack of medication and proper investigation, and no x-rays.

When I was an intern, there were some doctors who pretended to be religious. They pretended to have morals, to pray to God and to go to the mosque. When it came to the patients, they were very different – they put in no effort to help them. They were hypocrites: the ones appearing the most religious and moralistic were the worst at providing care for the patients.

There was a child of about six or seven who had been in a car accident. He was bleeding from the side and had a fracture. My colleague and I were the two in emergency and decided to call the orthopaedic registrar. He told us that he was just going off to prayer. I said that he needed to leave his prayers and come to the young patient. We did our best to keep the child alive until the doctor came out of his prayers. He turned up an hour later and took the child to theatre, but the child died. That was a horrible day for my colleague and me because that child would have lived if the surgeon had come over right away. Unfortunately, that was a regular occurrence in the hospital.

The hypocrisy of the prayers was offensive and upsetting. Other more relaxed doctors weren't interested in keeping up false appearances, and really put effort into helping patients. Later, when I took over the hospital, I tried to address those issues.

In 2001, after two years of internship, I started my training to become a specialist in internal medicine. At that time, my police check hadn't come back and I wondered if I'd be kicked out because of Naeem.

Talk of war was beginning to feature on the news. We were all blaming Saddam Hussein and thinking America would get rid of him – something to look forward to. Talking quietly in the doctors' accommodation, we believed it would be soon. However, nobody thought America would actually invade Iraq. And nobody foresaw the consequences and the trouble it would bring. We were counting the days and assumed that Saddam would just be removed.

The war started, and still no police check came through for me. I don't know what delayed it but I was able to continue my training. And once the war started, there were no more police checks.

A new relationship

In 2001, just after Naeem was executed, I developed a relationship with a girl. On my way to the hospital's sixth floor to find my friend Ahmed who was on call that day, and I saw a very pretty girl. She was slim, with white skin, and had a lovely smile. She was visiting a neighbour's child and asked me where the paediatric floor was, so I took her there.

Her name was Maha and she told me she was a teacher from a Sunni town. I gave her my phone number and she called me back three days later. Telling her I was interested in getting to know her, we started meeting in the university gardens where we would sit and talk.

Maha's family was a normal, conservative family which meant she couldn't go out with boys. We were dating in secret. If her family had found out, there would have been serious consequences – some families kill their daughters. They could have killed Maha and caused trouble for me. It is actually not related to religion but to culture, and mainly for the honour of the family. People are proud of honour and girls are regarded as the flag bearers of family honour. If the girl gets involved with a boy, the family's honour is stained and there's intense humiliation for the family.

Maha had two sisters and two brothers. When I called, I would ask for Ali. Ali was a code name because her brothers would have made trouble. I also had to call from a public phone because in those days we all used landlines and my number would have shown up. If her sisters answered the phone, they would get Maha but if her brothers answered, they would think it was a wrong number.

Maha's younger sister had cancer and was being treated at a paediatric hospital where chemotherapy wasn't available. At that time, I was working with an oncologist who had the authority to sign a prescription for chemotherapy. I could get chemotherapy for her from time to time.

The paediatric hospital was very close to my house, about two or three kilometres away. One rainy day, I decided to go by bus to visit Maha's sister. The road was soon under half a metre of water so I walked the last part. I was the only visitor that day. Later, a lady told Maha that I had walked in the rain and it showed her how much love was there. Sadly, Maha's sister died of cancer later on.

At times, Maha and I went out for lunch and to a tourist area called Baghdad Island where there was a lake. We had a good time together there.

In 2003, our relationship wasn't great because we couldn't see much of each other. Even though we fought a lot over the phone, I still loved her but things just didn't progress. Because of the war, all the landlines were gone and I couldn't really contact Maha for more than a year. When the landlines were fixed, I phoned her and she told me she was going to be at my hospital because one of her sisters was there to have a baby. If I wanted to see her, she would be there.

After work, I waited for a couple of hours in the afternoon but couldn't see her. Asking around, I discovered that her father had been killed in an explosion and as soon as Maha's sister had delivered, they'd left.

Taking a taxi to Maha's house, I entered a Sunni area. At that time, because of the civil war, no Shi'a in his right mind would normally do that. It was an extremely dangerous thing to do. But that didn't deter me. I had to find out what the situation was between Maha and me.

The funeral was to be in the late afternoon, so I went and sat there. Iraqi funerals are held in a big tent with chairs lined up inside. The tent is only for the men, the women go inside the house. People arrive from early morning till late afternoon, drink tea and coffee, and pay their respects.

Nobody knew me, so I was asked who I was. I lied, telling the men that my wife was one of Maha's friends and had gone to the hospital to see her and her sister. Unable to find them, my 'wife' was told of Maha's father's death and had sent me to pay respects. I had to come up with something and get away because they would have killed me had they known I was both Shi'a, and Maha's boyfriend.

I heard nothing from Maha until 2006. At two in the morning, the phone rang and it was Maha. She immediately started crying and I sensed that she was reaching out. Perhaps she'd been beaten by her husband, or just needed to talk. Hakeem was going crazy shouting at me to hang up because he had to sleep and I couldn't hear a thing. I never found out why she'd called, and never heard from her again.

Escaping Iraq

During 2002 and 2003, four of my friends were able to escape Iraq. In 2002, my friend Berbouti was the first to leave. He had a brother in America who helped him apply for immigration; he had to find a way to get out of Iraq because doctors weren't allowed to travel overseas.

Berbouti gave US$12,000 to the university and they allowed him to go for an overseas holiday. He'd found a law which allowed him to obtain a passport and travel between semesters. He came from a wealthy family who helped him with the money. The night before Berbouti left, the twelve of us, friends from medical school, stayed up in the street and saw him off with many sad tears at seven in the morning. He is now a GP in Canada.

This photo was taken at Dr Berbouti's farewell. He was the first of us to escape from Saddam's Iraq.

The second friend, Zaid, a Christian, left a few months after Berbouti. Using the same law, he pulled the same trick. Born in England, he was eligible for an English passport. While living in Iraq, he was forced to say that he was born in Baghdad, but his birth certificate showed otherwise. Again, we waited in the street overnight to say our sad goodbyes. Going to Syria, he contacted the British Embassy, obtained a passport and went to England. He's now a radiologist in Canada.

Our third friend paid a large sum of money to get a passport without mentioning his profession. Tim left on 18 March, two days before the war started. He couldn't wait any longer so had been willing to pay that enormous amount of money. Shortly after Tim left, we heard that the President of the United States gave Saddam Hussein forty-eight hours to leave the country or war would commence. Tim is now an emergency physician in the United Kingdom.

The fourth friend, Mohammed, travelled to Jordan at the end of 2002 before the war started. I don't know how he managed to gain his passport. The day after he left he emailed and told us he was in Jordan. He went to Japan, did a PhD and went to America to train to become a physician.

All my friends dreamed of leaving. All of them were financially able – some were wealthy, others were not badly off, but they could afford to leave. They all left the country illegally because it was the only way. I always assumed that, for me, leaving the country wasn't possible because I had no money, so I didn't think about it. Out of my twelve friends only one, Ali Amer, the head of our group, is still in Iraq. He is a surgeon on the front line with the Iraqi army. I have a photo of him in uniform in front of a helicopter.

Ali is a great person, one that we should all be looking to emulate. He's exceptional, always putting others ahead of himself. An entirely giving person, he was voted head of the Students' Union because his attitude and behaviour transcended any divide. With a sharp sense of humour, he exudes charisma.

The only one of us to stay on in Iraq, Ali felt he should stay where he was most needed. He used to send us photos of the action in hotspots like Mosul, Fallujah and Tikrit where he was saving lives of the military and civilian casualties. The images weren't about publicising his courage. He only shared them with his colleagues and close friends. That's how he is – quiet and brave.

Ali Amer, surgeon on the frontlines at Mosul, 2017

He even found humour in the middle of a battle when a senior army officer who was shot near his bottom objected when Ali told him that he had to examine it. 'But I'm the commander,' the officer said. 'I still need to examine your bottom,' Ali replied. 'Commander or not.'

He's no longer on the front line, thank God. But he's still working hard as a surgeon and now has a son. I tell him he's changed a lot. At university he was into body-building, he had long hair and very fair skin for an Iraqi. He looked exactly like Sylvester Stallone. Not anymore.

Operation Iraqi Freedom

When George W. Bush, the United States president, gave Saddam Hussein forty-eight hours to leave the country, no one believed he would go, nor believed that war would begin in two days. We listened to BBC radio then, not Voice of America. We didn't have satellite dishes in Iraq and if the police found one in the house, it meant prison. When President Bush and the United Kingdom's Prime Minister Tony Blair announced on the radio that Saddam had weapons of mass destruction, we believed it, because Saddam always bragged about things like that.

The United Nations Security Council sent in a committee to look for weapons. Saddam gave them a lot of information and weapons, but he wasn't someone anyone trusted. We naturally assumed he'd be hiding something because he thought he was smarter than everyone else.

In preparation for the war, the hospital divided us into three groups. Once the war started, each group would come in on a different day. I was in group C. The war started early in the morning on 20 March 2003; we could hear the missiles raining down. Changing into my work clothes, I had breakfast and took the bus to the hospital. It wasn't frightening because it was only missiles, not fighting in the streets.

At eight in the morning, I saw all the doctors were watching Saddam Hussein reading a statement on TV. He was wearing very thick glasses for the first time and calling the battle to come *marakat al hawasim*, meaning 'the decisive battle'.

Every day there were air attacks, so most of my friends, the interns and I remained at the hospital, staying close to the emergency department to help the injured.

The first two missile attacks were on Saddam Hussein Palace and a house in a very wealthy area of Baghdad because they thought Saddam was hiding there. The Americans were mainly targeting him. I think about forty-five missiles were launched against places where Saddam and his family were thought to be hiding, without anyone injured on the first day.

Later, we had civilian injuries from Iraqi forces trying to shoot down American planes with missiles that were very old; many didn't work properly, exploding in the wrong places. The injuries weren't too severe, but the Americans were also bombarding the Iraqi army and Republican Guard bases, sending many casualties to us.

That first day of war injuries, the hospital was in chaos, with doctors panicked and disorganised. After we finished working on the injured, we all sat down and were joined by a very old surgeon, Dr Wisam, who'd been in the Iraqi army as a military doctor. He was a communist, educated, smart, and taught us how to be organised.

We were all so young, some only one or two years out of medical school – I was three years out. We sat and listened to Dr Wisam and followed his instructions. He became like a godfather to us. He changed the way we dealt with a patient, so that we developed organisational skills. Rather than up to five doctors jumping in trying to help each new patient, one or two doctors helped each other. We also started to learn from our mistakes, doing things better. Our godfather never left the emergency department and his timely tuition saved many lives.

We were full of adrenaline and courageous. All the doctors around us were our friends. We'd danced together, studied together, graduated together, and then supported each other like a tightly knit family. When we finished our long shifts, we'd go to our rooms and Ali would make us laugh by pointing at Saddam's big photo and saying, 'There's not much time left for you!'

One day, coming back from the café after dinner, we saw that someone, probably one of the doctors, had thrown juice all over Saddam's photo. In the past, nobody would have dared do that. We were very apprehensive because the Ba'ath Party could have found out and had us killed.

One of the older doctors told us not to talk about the incident because we didn't want to be the last people executed. He told us to wait. There was a feeling that the 'time was coming'. There were also a few doctors who supported Saddam so we tried to avoid publicly talking about what happened.

Saddam's supporters were not good doctors. They were unethical and had no empathy with the patients. Nobody liked them and even if they did occasionally do something for the good, it wasn't seen by anyone I knew. They were dangerous because they could drop a word somewhere and get us into serious strife.

We worked continuously for three weeks, but then on 3 April as I was going to the hospital, I found that all public transport had stopped. When I eventually got to the hospital, there were only six doctors and the place was not running so, after a while, I decided to head back home.

It was a very dark evening, and I walked via a Shi'a holy shrine close to the hospital. About fifty thousand people usually visit the shrine each day but that night I was alone. It felt like I was the last person on earth. After praying at the shrine, I continued towards home. The only people I saw were some of Saddam's volunteers. They were dangerous people, so I was pleased that nobody stopped or talked to me.

A few days later, the Americans arrived and took Baghdad airport. They were very close. In the last week of the war, Saddam Hussein brought his army about one hundred metres from our house, filling the parks and gardens where we had played soccer as children. Aiming to attack the airport from there, he placed his tanks among the civilians, using the people as human shields.

By 7 April, most people in my town left their houses and escaped from Baghdad. Only a few families remained, including mine. About 25 metres away across the road was a house with a generator. Because of the lack of electricity, the family would ask the ordinary soldiers to go in and have a cup of tea. The soldiers were conscripts and not necessarily followers of Saddam. As it turned out, the Americans were watching what was going on.

At seven o'clock that morning I was in the kitchen having breakfast with my mother, intending to go to the hospital. An American plane flew in low and attacked the town. Many houses were hit including ours, and the house of the neighbour with the generator took a direct attack. The Americans probably thought a senior army officer was there, or it was headquarters or something like that.

My mother pulled me by my neck, taking me under the stairs to a small shelter. A shell penetrated the kitchen ceiling where I'd been standing, making a big hole. My mother saved my life.

Hakeem brought the car to the front of our house, and while all my family got in, I heard my neighbours with the generator calling out that they had injuries. There were hundreds of cluster bombs in the area between our house and the neighbour. Without thinking, I ran across the road with my first aid kit. Cluster bombs are very small, I didn't look at the ground to see them but I must have stepped on so many, as the road was filled with them. I don't know why they didn't explode on me. I was lucky – or protected by God.

Two of my neighbours had been shot in the legs, were severely injured and were bleeding everywhere. As I helped them, another neighbour told me he had a car and would take them to the hospital. Wearing just my track suit, we took off to a hospital he knew, but we soon found that the road was blocked. Suggesting my hospital instead, we turned around and sped there. Arriving in emergency, friends working there asked me what I was doing. 'The Americans fucked us,' I said. I was clearly in shock as I don't normally speak like that.

My colleagues told me that they'd been working for forty-eight hours in emergency without being relieved – I realised that the hospital had begun working again the day after I'd left. Twenty doctors for over 200 badly injured people. I told my colleagues that I'd find something to wear and work with them.

Borrowing a friend's jeans and finding a white coat, I joined my colleagues. I had not realised what a terrible day it would be for all of us – for me, for my neighbours. All the patients were from the attack on my town and I knew most of them. Without enough beds, we tended the injured on the floor, jumping from one to the other to help.

Around midday, things had settled with no new patients coming in, so we were able to grab a bite to eat. By seven that night, I still had no idea what had happened to my family or where they had gone – but I stayed on working at the hospital with my friends.

Later, I realised the US military were using cluster bombs, bombs containing a lot of small bombs which cover a large area when dropped: a prohibited weapon by international law. When the bomb senses heat, sound and movement it explodes. So many houses in my town were destroyed by them.

Cluster bombs

The cluster bombings were reported widely by the media, and I saw many injuries from them. Canadian reporter Robert J. Galbraith took photographs of cluster bomb injuries, collating them in his book *Iraq: Eyewitness to War* (Hushion House, 2005). There's a famous one of a nine-year-old boy who'd lost his eye from one of these bombs. I'd taken Mr Galbraith to see patients; my photo ended up in his book.

After a group of journalists came to the hospital asking about the cluster bombs, I took them to my home town to show them what remained of my home and others. Because there was some talk of compensation for people affected by the bombs, people came out of their homes and were calling out to me. I told them that the visit wasn't about compensation but about the bombs.

One old man's house was burnt and blackened so we went there, and also to a house just in front of ours where there was an unexploded cluster bomb in the roof. We went to the neighbour's house where I'd helped the two injured people, and we found some unexploded cluster bombs still there. Eventually a volunteer who knew how to dismantle bombs removed them. He was a very brave man who selflessly helped the community. Later, some bombs exploded while he was working on them: I don't know whether he was just injured or killed.

It was very frustrating and upsetting seeing the cluster bomb injuries. Many children were killed, others permanently maimed, suffering blindness or loss of limbs. Sometimes the injuries were so bad, I couldn't imagine how they would recover. And, if they did, how would they survive with such loss.

We had no time to discuss the injuries that came our way because there would be more the next day, and the next, and the next. More of the same and many new ones. Sometimes we got to discuss the very worst back at the doctors' accommodation, like the day when a young lady who had her stomach, bowels and some of her lung blown out in an explosion came to the hospital. She was still conscious and aware, but there was nothing we could do for her. She was dying in front of us. It was difficult for us all to talk about. Even now, I find it hard to think about it.

We all suffered post-traumatic stress disorder. Manifesting itself in the years after the war, I became severely depressed, although I still managed to work. It seemed normal – yet it wasn't. All the doctors suffered this way.

In 2005 and 2006, the Iraqi militia would use ambulances if they were coming to take and murder one of our doctors. We were always frightened when they turned up. So the first few years in Australia were bad: hearing an ambulance would strike me with fear and I'd have palpitations. Loud sounds and fireworks would unnerve me to the point where I thought I might not be able to work. It took time but I eventually came to terms with it and now live a normal life.

The authority of one

It was after midnight on that long day of bombing when we finally got to sleep. The following day one of my friends went to the director's office and stole the antenna from his TV for ours so we could watch what was happening. We saw Saddam's statue being torn down by Iraqi civilians, helped by American soldiers.

Along with the director, there were only twenty-three doctors at the hospital. We were all watching TV because nothing was happening in the emergency department. It was taking a lot of effort to topple Saddam's statue and I was cheering before I realised that there were two guys from the Ba'ath party in reception. If they'd heard me I could have been shot.

That night we could see American troops running around the freeway at the back of the hospital. Later on, we were sitting in the doctors' accommodation when we saw people coming to the College of Law, part of Saddam University. They were Iraqis, looting and burning the college. People thought that because it was called Saddam University, it was related to Saddam, but, in fact, it was just a college. We watched with sadness, believing the entire university – somewhere we'd spent years studying with many colleagues – would be burnt to the ground. We hardly slept that night.

On the morning of 9 April, the last day of the war, I was up at seven, and changed into my white coat to go to the emergency department. I intended to fit in a visit to the College of Medicine to say goodbye to it before it was destroyed. Arriving at Emergency, there were no doctors in attendance so I stayed in case any patients turned up. One casualty came in with a bullet injury to the abdomen. I did his blood group match then called the surgical team to let them know we had a case for surgery.

At seven-thirty, a doctor rostered to work in Emergency appeared and I was able to walk over to the university to say my goodbyes. Springtime flowers were blooming, and it seemed peaceful for the time being. The library and cafeteria were locked but I was happy just to see where my friends and I used to sit for all those years.

Heading back towards the hospital, I came across some armed Iraqi civilians in the college grounds. I asked them what they were doing. They recognised my doctor's status by my white coat and happily told me they were there to protect the university from looters. Thanking them profusely, I continued back to Emergency.

Outside the hospital I then saw around forty people holding guns and shouting a religious slogan, 'Ya Hussain'. Again, invoking the perceived authority of the white coat, I asked them what they were doing there. They said they'd all come to protect the hospital. Telling them it wouldn't work if they kept shouting slogans, I advised them to find two older people to be their representatives and bring them to me.

As two elderly gentlemen came along, I spotted an engineer who worked at the hospital and asked him to find me a room in the engineering department, which happened to be right next door to emergency. Sitting the gentlemen down, I told them that if the group wanted to protect the hospital, they had to be organised into two twelve-hour shifts every twenty-four hours. Each one of them would be responsible for a group and would be the ones designated to talk to me. The two groups would be divided into eight smaller sections of five people with a leader for each who would report to them. There had to be eight groups because we had four corners around the university and four corners around the hospital. They agreed.

The elders told me that they didn't have enough weapons. That was an easy fix because the Ba'ath Party who had worked at the hospital had a lot of weapons that they had abandoned when they escaped. After distributing the weapons, we sent some of the new guards home so they could return for the later shifts.

The Saddam Hussein Hospital was well armed because Saddam had had a very well-equipped hospital inside his palace. Thinking that it would be targeted by the Americans, Saddam evacuated all the staff and equipment to the newly built four-storey section attached to our hospital. Everyone attached to that unit escaped on 8 April leaving all the equipment behind.

Just before the fall of Baghdad, the army had been posted to the centre of towns and had then abandoned their weapons in the streets. Military bases were also abandoned and raided by civilians for weapons. It meant that weapons were everywhere. Thankfully, ammunition was expensive and difficult to obtain so the situation had become less lethal.

Leaving the group of guards, I found Dr Wisam, the older surgeon who had taught us to be organised. He was very upset and told me bitterly that the doctors were leaving the hospital. Apparently, word was getting around that the university was being burnt down and the hospital would be next. Explaining to him that I'd arranged full protection for both institutions, I convinced him to see all the doctors and implore them not to leave.

As it was quiet in emergency, I let Dr Wisam know that I wanted to go home briefly later in the day to check on my family. 'Make sure you come back,' he told me. 'I'm relying on you now.'

About three, I left the hospital to take the one-hour walk home. Reaching a major intersection I could see four American tanks sitting in the middle of a huge roundabout surrounded by a thousand or more Iraqi civilians – well, there may have been soldiers there but they wisely wouldn't have been in uniform any longer.

American soldiers were sitting on the tanks just staring silently at the people who silently and curiously stared back. There was no interaction between the two groups; it would have been the first time that many Iraqis had seen foreigners. The American troops were very young and sweating. Holding my white coat, I walked between the tanks. Nobody said anything to me and I went on my way thinking the situation most bizarre and a little funny.

As I walked I saw people looting a government factory. People were coming out carrying things and filling their cars. They were simply stealing from the government.

Continuing towards home – and keeping my white coat clearly visible – I heard a car pull up beside me. The driver had noticed my coat and vented his anger and frustration at the looting. He was upset that people would turn to stealing so quickly. I offered him some money to give me a lift home, but he refused it and took me without payment.

Relieved to find my mother and Hakeem safe in the house, I had a meal, showered, changed my clothes and an hour later walked back to the hospital. Keeping to the quieter streets and avoiding the main intersection, I was able to return safely to the hospital before sunset.

That morning, one of our twelve good friends, Mushtaq, had been working with us. We were without nurses, so he'd stepped up to change the dressings for all two hundred patients we had in the wards. Spending several minutes on each injury, it took him many hours, so he also went home briefly to check on his family. Spending four hours walking to and from his home, he came back exhausted and very distressed. He'd seen a patient he'd treated looting the government building. The sight had shocked him.

Protecting the hospital

At ten that night, a guard protecting the building came to take me by car to see how the checkpoints were doing. The American army had imposed a curfew from nine and it was very dark outside. Being still on hospital grounds we were able to get safely to each checkpoint, so it didn't matter that we couldn't be out on the roads and subject to the curfew.

I took the names of every checkpoint guard and praised them for volunteering to protect the hospital and university. I would do nothing with the names, but I was now their commander and my duty was to encourage them at every opportunity. They were all from low socio-economic families living near the hospital. Because I came from a similar area and background we understood and related to each other easily. Leaving their homes during the war to protect the hospital was selfless and courageous, and ultimately saved the hospital.

My colleagues from higher socio-economic groups had never met people like our new guards and were fearful of them. The guards also hadn't related well with the doctors in the past. I was fortunate that I could understand their humour and mannerisms and talk easily with them. Our skin colour was also similar and, of course, the white coat always helped. That white coat had great standing with the Iraqi people, as doctors were so highly respected.

People from the south of Iraq, like my family, are predominantly Shi'a and usually have darker skin. They were kept in near-poverty by Saddam and his regime, and were denied education and good employment opportunities. Very few Shi'a from the south lived in the better towns or were well-placed in government like the lighter-skinned Sunni.

My darker skin and the fact that I was studying to be a doctor enabled me to mingle with both sides. Being in the middle helped me to understand both demographics. When talking to the guards, I could use their language rather than talking down to them. I knew how they felt and how they talked because of how and where I grew up. They respected me a great deal for that.

Returning from the checkpoints, I was met by the two elders, who told me that Ali Wa'idh, a representative of the Grand Ayatollah (the highest Shi'a Muslim religious figure in the world) wanted to meet me. He'd been under house arrest for twenty-two years and, with Saddam gone, had just emerged. I'd never heard of him, but he was in command and, although I didn't know it, had sent the volunteers to guard the hospital in the first place.

To meet such a figure was a very high honour. When we finished at the hospital about ten that night, I went with the volunteer guards to a small house in a nearby town. Luckily, the Americans weren't around to find us violating the curfew. Ali Wa'idh's son met us and took us to a white-faced man with a very big beard. All the men I was with kissed his hand, but I shook it, trying to distance myself from his power and authority, and to stay out from under his command.

Asking me to sit, he told me that wanted to meet me because he'd heard so much about my remaining in the emergency department full-time and always helping people.

I called him Sayyid, a title that means descended from the prophets, and told him that I didn't pray to God and I didn't follow or practise religion. This was a strategic lie because, again, it slipped me a little further from under his control. In fact, I am a religious person, but I keep this mostly to myself. I pray regularly but it is a private thing – I believe religion is a direct relationship between a person and God, and should always be kept like this. I rebel against the use of religion to gain advantage. My way of practicing religion is to feel that God is watching me all the time and to do the best I can to be good.

I let Ali Wa'idh know that I was concerned about the hospital and the university being looted and, for the hundreds of patients' sakes, wanted the guards to continue working. He asked me what I thought would work.

I told him that his people could protect the hospital from the outside – anything outside the hospital to the door of the emergency department should be their responsibility. The door of the emergency department was also the entry to the hospital, so anything from inside the door of the emergency department would be my responsibility. I offered to be accountable and liable for anything that happened like theft or damage inside the hospital.

Ali Wa'idh was agreeable to all of that so I mentioned that recovering patients were upset at seeing weapons being carried inside the hospital by the volunteer guards. In fact, it concerned the doctors more than the patients. The volunteers were untrained and ill-educated, and the doctors feared that if they were angry or over-excited, they may shoot indiscriminately. Ali Wa'idh agreed with that too – and anything he agreed with became law.

Responsibility of the hospital

In a surprise move, Ali Wa'idh then asked me to become the director of the hospital. I told him I was a very junior doctor, and that no consultants would come and work at a hospital run by me. I said that although the present director was corrupt before the war he'd never left the hospital during it. He was a surgeon and had been the only consultant to stay with the junior doctors for those twelve days of war. The director had sat and talked to us junior doctors, and seeing him as more human we began to like him. Although we had disliked him intensely before, there was now a bond forming.

I advised Ali Wa'idh that if we kept the consultant – an older and respected orthopaedic surgeon – then other consultants would come to work at the hospital. If the hospital was running successfully, it would help keep looters away.

By the meeting's end, I had become responsible for the inside of the hospital – liability, finances, everything. Everything outside was the responsibility of the guards.

The first instruction I gave when I got back was that anyone leaving the hospital, including myself, would be searched. With so much equipment and money inside the hospital, I didn't want any more of it stolen. It became a routine and even the director was checked. At first, the director was upset when he was included, but I told him that these were my instructions and no one was exempt.

The first day after my meeting with Ali Wa'idh, the guards caught eleven people trying to steal from the hospital. The guards called me in to deal with a well-dressed man who appeared to be educated and in a good job. He'd stolen some lettuce, rice and lentils and I wondering why he'd do such a thing. I was embarrassed for him and it was difficult to look him in the eye. Angry with him, I told the guards to send all the items to the kitchen because we needed the food for the patients and the doctors. Then I told the man to go home and never come back. He left in his very nice car. He was lucky the guards didn't shoot him.

Sometimes, the guards went a bit crazy. One night around midnight, they called to say they'd caught someone carrying a grenade and threatening to kill us. In fact, the man was a drug addict and not in his own mind. I had to get him away from the guards because they were throwing him around violently. I felt sorry for him and could see that the manhandling could easily end up with him being shot. The guards assured me that he was dangerous, but I could see that he wasn't, and that it was the guards who were excitable and over-zealous.

In front of the hospital, Saddam's people had stupidly dug a lot of bunkers from which they intended to fight the Americans. That was before they all ran away. Realising that I had to put on an act to save our drug addict, I told the guards to throw him into one of the bunkers. I then asked a guard for his AK-47 and started to act insanely angry, yelling at the guy, frightening him out of his wits and telling him I was about to shoot him. The guards were shocked at my extreme behaviour and begged me not to. 'Don't do this doctor!' they cried out. 'Don't shoot him!'

I then told the addict that because of the guards, I had decided to release him but if I saw him around the hospital again I would shoot him myself. Calling me 'sir' over and over, he thanked me and ran off.

The guards had weapons and they were protecting the hospital but at the same time they were not regulated or trained, so it was possible that they would shoot without understanding the consequences.

Within the next couple of days, it became obvious that I controlled the guards. The doctors started to call them Issam's peshmerga, peshmerga being the name of the Kurdish militia. The hospital was running, people were working, the doctors were coming and going, and things were running smoothly.

Everyone was happy – except our director.

The director's power challenge

On 13 April Dr Hakam, the director, told me that he wanted the guards gone and he would bring in American troops. He said he would go to the American army and ask them to protect the hospital. He wouldn't accept the guards because they were different and he felt they didn't respect him. They were common people and he was regarded as one of Saddam's followers. In particular, he was upset at having to be checked in and out of the hospital. He had lost his power.

According to Dr Hakam, he had gone to the American base and the Americans had told him they would send the troops a few days later. The troops arrived with twenty-two tanks. They entered the hospital and told the director they had come to protect it. The director's immediate reaction was to go to the guards, call them all thieves and tell them to leave the hospital. It became a power play.

Two of my doctor friends talked to the American troops and were told that the troops weren't in fact there to protect the hospital, rather they were there to protect a very high-ranking army officer who would be visiting. It was the leader of the US troops in Baghdad, and the soldiers had come ahead of his planned arrival later in the day at which time he would talk to the director and hand over medical supplies from Kuwait. Once he left, the troops would also leave.

I told the guards not to leave and went to the director with the chief resident of the junior doctors. He ordered us to see the Head of the College of Medicine with him.

The Head of the College, Dr Riaydh, was the director's superior and head of both the college and the hospital. When the three of us entered his office, Dr Hakam started shouting at me to take my thieves and get out of the hospital. When I asked him who would protect the hospital if the guards left, he said he'd spoken to the Americans two days previously and that they would protect the hospital. I then told him that the information was not accurate.

Still treating the director with respect, I informed him that the American troops had come to prepare for the top American military commander to visit him. At that point, the director didn't know that. I then told Dr Riaydh that the director had been the only consultant to stay at the hospital for the whole twelve days of the war. I asked why the Head of the College had left him working alone.

The director then became very angry, hitting the table and telling Riaydh that it was true that he was left by himself. Clearly, I had inadvertently made trouble between them. Dr Hakam told Riaydh that he was taking leave for a week to have a holiday; we all turned to leave but Dr Riaydh asked me to stay. He then asked me to keep the guards. When I told him that there were only twenty-three doctors in the hospital and we weren't getting any help or any money, he asked where he should get the money. I said, 'Use your own!'

At that, Riaydh gave me 750,000 Iraqi dinars for the doctors who'd stayed on during the war. Then I told him that I had no title in the hospital to manage the guards. To do my job I needed legitimacy and an official position. He agreed. It was win-win. I avoided a fight with the director, we kept the guards, and there was money for the doctors. Surprisingly, when I told the doctors about the money they were upset, telling me they didn't want it: they wanted recognition.

Americans in the hospital

After the visit with Riaydh, I was walking outside the hospital close to the emergency department when the guards brought some Americans to see me – a General and a Colonel. The General was responsible for Baghdad. He wanted to know if I was responsible for the hospital and I told him I was. I asked what was wrong. He told me that my guards would not let his troops enter the hospital with weapons. I laughed and told him that I'd made the direction that nobody was allowed to bring weapons inside the hospital.

The General pointed to a pistol strapped to his leg and asked about that one. I told him it would be fine. He then ordered all his troops to leave their weapons and asked if there was somewhere he could sit and talk with me. I asked the guards to prepare a meeting room and walked between the General and the Colonel into the emergency department. It was wonderful to see no weapons being carried in there. We had rules and regulations that were helping to create a smoothly running and safe environment.

Inside the conference room, three of my doctor friends and I sat on couches with the General and Colonel. People from a TV station were recording the conference, as I informed the General that we needed things like oxygen and electricity, and we didn't have enough clean water.

The General replied that he had brought some gifts from the Kuwaiti government – IV fluids, needles, syringes and lots of useful supplies like that.

When we finished and shook hands, the General and Colonel started to leave, but I was stopped by the TV people who wanted an interview. They asked me what my position was, because I was very young at twenty-seven to be running a hospital. I told them that I had no title, but my friends called me Mr President. It was a silly thing to say but it was just typical Iraqi humour.

Then, asked what the hospital's name would be if it was to change from Saddam Hussein Teaching Hospital, I told them, 'Issam University Teaching Hospital.' An absolutely absurd response and I'm sure that would have prevented it going to air. But, who knows?

Mr Prisoner

The guards were always volatile and unpredictable. On one occasion I was inside the hospital when I heard gunfire and people shouting, 'We want Issam and Dr Imad!'

The guards had some sort of extreme grievance with Imad and me, so we closed all the doors and went to the doctors' accommodation. I heard that the guards were accusing me of stealing and wanted to see me.

Not realising how serious the situation was, I said that I'd go out to them. The older doctors told me to forget about going out and leave it to them. They were genuinely concerned that I'd be shot. A group of five doctors volunteered to approach the guards to find out what was going on.

The parties agreed that a representative of Ali Wa'idh would come to the hospital and discuss the accusation with me inside the doctors' accommodation. Only one of the guards would be present at this meeting, as a representative. I told the doctors that I had no problems with that.

The religious representative was wearing a suit and was accompanied by a guard. I joined them in the place where we usually watched TV. There were at least thirty doctors assembled there and they were frightened. I chose to remain standing.

I told the religious representative that before we discussed anything, I wanted him to know that I had the master key to the hospital. I let him know that I had taken responsibility for the hospital under the approval of Ali Wa'idh. Then I handed him the key, telling him that I was no longer able to take responsibility. There was a condition – my tribe and I were of the same religious persuasion as Ali Wa'idh, and I wanted anyone who accused me of stealing to bring before him the evidence so that Ali Wa'idh could judge. I would accept any decision Ali Wa'idh made.

However, if the accusers failed to prove I had stolen anything, my tribe would punish the accusers. That was the law of the tribe in Iraq. In actual fact, my tribe is very peaceful and not powerful, but these people didn't know that. I was ready to challenge the accusers with religious and tribal law because there was no government. If they failed to prove anything there would be consequences. It was quite a bluff.

The hospital had millions of dollars' worth of equipment, so by offering the representative the key I was showing that I didn't care for the riches of the hospital. The representative reasoned that if I had stolen something I would not have offered him the key, because a thief would not let go of a good source of supply so easily. That offer convinced him that I hadn't stolen anything. When I asked him about the guards, he told me not to worry and that he would sort them out. With that, we re-opened the emergency department and went back to work. There was no investigation. I still didn't really know what I was supposed to have stolen or why the guards were so upset. From then on, the doctors changed my name from 'Mr President' to 'Mr Prisoner'.

A few days later, I asked one of the guards what it was all about. He told me that it was all just a test. That was a hard test, I thought to myself, and I still have no clue as to what the real story was. It didn't change me; I would still go and check on the guards and occasionally have meals with them.

Tribal system

Everybody in Iraq belongs to a tribe. The tribes are predominantly from the southern and western parts of Iraq; less so in Baghdad.

It's not written in law but if someone from another tribe attacks me, my tribe can ask for compensation. If compensation isn't given, my tribe could kill or hurt someone from the other tribe. Some tribes are very strong, and wars can start from very simple things.

Insulting someone means trouble.

When I was accused of stealing, it was an insult. When I said I came from a tribe, I was sending the message that I didn't come from nowhere, even though I was from Baghdad where tribes are less common. On that occasion, there were no police or regular laws there to protect me, so I used the threat of tribal law. They were just words to help me to get away from the trouble I was in. It wouldn't have worked if put to the test, but when you tell people you will use tribal law it makes them think twice. They don't want to go there. They didn't have any evidence, so they withdrew the accusation.

If you commit an offence against someone from another tribe, your tribe will not support you and you will be left exposed to the other tribe's retribution. The leadership of the tribe is handed down from generation to generation through one family, but we all have the same ancestors. We are all cousins, brothers or otherwise related.

Tribal people commonly all live in one area, although in the 60s and 70s a lot of people left the countryside and came to Baghdad. There it's not the one tribe – it's a different mix. Different tribes have their own way of doing things too. For example, I can say you insulted me, and I can be compensated by you giving me three of your daughters. That happens a lot. I remember one guy was married to three ladies on the one day as tribal compensation.

It's such a shame. It's supposed to stop the bloodshed of tribes going to war, but the law is misused a lot. The penalties can be very severe. These days people will go to the tribe for simple things, and it causes a lot of trouble. For example, when a patient dies from old age, the relatives could accuse the doctor of killing the patient. They demand that the doctor pay compensation.

During Saddam's time, the use of tribal law was low. Saddam would not allow people to do their own thing. Now the tribes predominate again, and some are powerful.

Medicines for the hospital

Around that time, two men came to see me. They were looking after a warehouse where a lot of medicines were stored and were afraid that they'd be stolen. They knew I was running the hospital and they wanted for us to come and take whatever we could use.

I went in an ambulance with a friend and a Jordanian from the Red Cross. The warehouse was in a mainly Sunni area of Baghdad and there were Sunni volunteers with long beards doing the same sort of job as the Shi'a guards at our hospital. It was good to see. Entering the warehouse, we were confronted by enormous quantities of medicines that Saddam had hidden from us. We had suffered terribly because of lack of supply and yet everything we needed had been right here.

We filled the ambulance with all kinds of antibiotics and every medication we needed: it would have easily been valued at twenty million dinars. I signed the documents to take receipt of the hoard, and we managed to do two trips. It was a great coup and people were so pleased to see an ambulance with a white-coated doctor and Red Cross member travelling the streets. They waved to us happily.

On one of the trips, we stopped by my house because it was on the way. My friends and I had lunch there, the ambulance sitting out the front, full of millions of dollars of medicines.

At the hospital I used two storage areas for the medicines. One was the big conference room, the other was an unused room near the radiology department. I had some of my twelve good friends helping to sort the big boxes according to contents and quantities. It was heavy work, and I remember one of the guys, who is now a neurosurgeon in America, naked except for his underwear at one o'clock in the morning, lifting those heavy

Medicines for the hospital

boxes. We had to get things in order ourselves because there were no pharmacists back working.

Myself and a friend would supply the hospital departments with the antibiotics and injections they needed. The pharmacy wasn't working in emergency so one of my doctor friends would sit there, and doctors would come along and ask for what they needed. Everything was recorded in writing. Everyone started to pay a simple sum, maybe fifty cents for each item. The money was given to me to keep track of, so I became responsible for finances as well.

Every day I would get up at seven in the morning and wouldn't be finished until one o'clock the next morning. I was still part of the medical team to see patients in the wards and had shifts in the emergency department as part of my roster. I wasn't able to sleep at home for two months but I did visit a few times; once with an interpreter, once with a journalist, and once with the ambulance. They were the only times I saw my family.

I was also liaising with a humanitarian organisation which was bringing food to the hospital every three days. They were very good. I don't know who told them how much to bring but they brought 53 kilos of potatoes, and the same of tomatoes, onions and oranges. I still don't know why they chose 53 kilos of each. As I was responsible for receiving the supplies and for their distribution, I took the produce to the kitchens and told the staff there that a certain amount was for the patients and a certain amount was for the doctors.

There was one incident with the kitchen staff. I had three-and-a-half bags of oranges delivered and told the kitchen staff that one bag was for the doctors and two-and-a-half bags were for the patients. That evening as I was doing the ward rounds, I asked the patients how they were and if they enjoyed their orange. I was most upset when everyone answered that they'd had no orange.

I had agreed with the religious leader that the hospital was my responsibility, and that there would be justice and fairness and no stealing. I was liable for everything in the hospital, including each orange. I went immediately to the kitchen and demanded to know where the oranges were. Going to the storage area, I found the missing two-and-a-half bags that the staff were going to take out of the hospital.

This made me so angry. Iraqis are so corrupt and don't think twice before stealing from their own people. They were like that before the war and they'll probably never change.

I saw a young boy who looked honest and told him to grab one of the bags as I put the other over my shoulder. We went around the wards distributing the oranges to everyone. As we did, I saw a patient who was a friend of my brother. He asked me what I was doing. When I told him, he took the bag and carried it for me while I passed out the fruit.

Conflict

When Saddam's people escaped from the hospital, they left behind two very new Land Cruisers. A couple of religious people with some connection to the guards came to the hospital and spoke with the director, telling him that they needed the vehicles for the public service of electricity. It was just an excuse to steal the cars.

Dr Hakam asked me to come to him, along with the chief resident. Entering the room, I saw that the religious people were leaving. One of them was a very powerful man with a lot of followers. Once they had left, Dr Hakam pulled out a gun and pointed it at me, telling me to take my thieves and leave the hospital. Apparently, he thought I'd set it up. I was surprised, but not afraid, and thinking fast, I asked him to explain. Dr Hakam told me the religious guys wanted to take the cars for a public service. I asked him to put the gun down and then asked him why he thought we would help them.

I told him that our doctors were also doing a public service and we also needed the cars for the hospital to bring food to the doctors. I gave him the excuse he needed in the same language as the religious people. He was Sunni and he didn't know the religious peoples' ways. He was convinced and put the gun down.

Dr Hakam wrote down that the hospital was allocating a car each to the chief resident and to me to use in the service of the hospital and gave the paper to me. That's how things were. There was a conflict inside the hospital and I was in the middle of it; I walked into a room and there was a gun in my face and I walked out of the room with a piece of paper and a car. They were interesting times!

Dr Imad, the chief resident, was looking at me and laughing. He is a Sunni but we worked well together. He asked me how I had managed that – it had been a really very difficult situation.

Every day, things would come up. There was a lot of conflict, but I was quickly learning how to deal with difficult situations. I now had the guards, the director of the hospital, people working in the kitchen and the doctors working with me.

After the war

After the war ended, things became more stable. Our hospital had been served by 450 doctors before the war and then only twenty-three doctors during the war; most of those who stayed were from Baghdad. We all knew each other, had been to the same university and had the same way of thinking. They told me I was an inspiration for them; they admired me and so they helped me. That was a very humbling thing to hear.

Other doctors were slowly drifting back to work. They were either from the south and had always been discriminated against by the government or were from the west and were mostly Saddam's people. Many of these doctors had a lot of anger against the government. They came back to the hospital and found me; I had the guards under me and I was the primary contact with Ali Wa'idh, the religious leader. My family and I were always joyous, opened-minded and didn't pretend to be overtly religious in our daily lives. These returning doctors looked down on me and questioned why I was the primary contact when I supposedly wasn't religious.

They met with the religious leader and told him I wasn't praying and asked him why he trusted me. Remember, I'd informed the religious leader when we first met that I wasn't praying. That had given me credibility. Ali Wa'idh became upset that these doctors were questioning my authority. He told the doctors that nobody could go to him except me. The doctors were not happy with that and refused to help me. Well, I thought, you can't make everyone happy, so I continued my work, ran the hospital as best I could, and made sure the patients were being looked after.

In the first few weeks after the end of the war, some of the guards came to see me. They were very upset, telling me that there was a pregnant lady who required a Caesarean section. She was being asked to pay fifty thousand dinars and like most people, she didn't have that sort of money. Before the war Saddam had applied a system where people paid for their hospital admission, and now the director had reintroduced the fee-paying system to anyone needing medical help.

Firstly, I saw the doctors and told them to go ahead with the procedure. Then I went to the religious leader who told me to negotiate the issue with the director. I had to go about it this way because I had another niggling problem. Two of Saddam's people were back at the hospital. One was the reception manager, a powerful figure who was constantly stirring up trouble between the doctors and the Americans. The other person was totally corrupt and worked in the finance department. They were both bad influences within the hospital.

I went to Dr Hakam and informed him that the religious leader had decided not to provide guards if the hospital imposed high fees on the people. I also told him that Ali Wa'idh wanted the reception manager and the finance guy out of the building. That day the admission fee was reduced to fifty cents and only applied in the emergency department.

From that time until I left Iraq in 2007, no patients were charged fees. Within two days, doctors from other big hospitals in Baghdad changed their systems and stopped the fees for patients. They were also young doctors like me. In the end, all the hospitals became free after the war. The change started with me at my hospital and it transformed it from a private to a public hospital in one day, lessening the burden on the people.

Unfortunately, the problem I had with the other returned doctors didn't resolve. I just carried on with my job. I was always pleasant despite the fact they treated me badly. They didn't stop me: I continued to work hard doing the things I believed in.

A trip out

About a month after the war, we were watching the news in the doctors' accommodation at the hospital one night at about nine o'clock. Two men came in and asked where Dr Issam was. I told them it was me, and one of them came over and tried to kiss my hand. Surprised, I asked him what he was doing and took him outside.

He told me that his brother had been shot in the right arm with a major blood vessel damaged. A tourniquet had been put on and he was told that if he didn't get treatment in the following six hours he would lose his arm. Someone had written the time on his forehead to indicate how much time the arm had. Telling me he'd gone to the hospital closest to his house and found no surgeon there, he'd gone to a second hospital some way away and had the same bad luck. Time was ticking away.

I headed straight to emergency, where the man's brother was on a trolley. I then went to see our surgeon who lived close by. After I described the problem, he told me that he had no surgical material to fix the artery and that the patient should be taken to the Medical City about fifty minutes away. Normally, this wouldn't have been an issue, but the Americans' curfew would start in fifteen minutes and they'd shoot at any ambulance on the street. It was quite a dilemma.

I went back to the ambulance guys, and asked them if they would drive the patient to the Medical City. They said they would but needed an English-speaking doctor with them in case they were caught by the Americans. I asked the on-call doctor to go with the ambulance but he was initially reluctant to go. He did agree, but as he was clearly frightened I decided to go myself rather than risking his life. I considered it to be my responsibility.

Thankfully, we missed the American patrols and made it to the hospital without incident. There, I asked for the vascular surgeon to attend and had another bit of luck. It was Dr Sabah, someone who I'd worked with a couple of years back. When I showed him the time on the patient's forehead, he told me that he'd already done thirteen operations that day and could barely stand with fatigue. However, because it was me asking, he said he'd do one more. Such luck!

I saw the patient's brother as I was coming back from the blood bank with some units of blood Dr Sabah needed for the operation. The brother wanted to give me money but I refused it, I felt sorry for the man whose brother who might lose his arm. I gave *him* ten thousand dinars instead. I knew he wasn't from Baghdad and wouldn't have family around to help. I suggested that he give some money to the ambulance drivers as a customary tip, but the drivers refused it, telling us they were doing it for God.

I made the brother promise to let me know if the patient's arm was saved. A few days later he found me at my hospital to report that the operation had been a success and the arm and hand were working again. He handed me a pile of small notes, telling me that because of the success of the operation he'd decided to bring back the money I'd given him. I shoved it into my pocket. I found out later that he'd given me twenty-five thousand dinars instead of the ten that I'd given him.

When I asked him how everything was going, he told me that they needed antibiotics because none were available at the hospital his brother was in. He'd been buying injections for three thousand dinars each and needed three each day. As I gave him five days' supplies, I noticed that a nurse was watching me. I wasn't trying to hide the fact – it was going to a patient who needed help. However, the nurse thought I was selling the drugs and told a doctor who particularly disliked me. That caused a few problems later on.

After two months, the hospital was running efficiently. All the doctors were back at work, there was no danger of stealing and things were improving. I decided to hold an election to hand over responsibility to a new chief resident of doctors and a vice chief resident. In the past, Saddam's people had appointed those positions – never a good thing.

I decided that the chief resident would be one of the doctors and anyone could nominate himself. I chose the committee from all the doctors who disliked me so that no one could say the election was rigged.

Handing over the job

There were 120 junior doctors who all loved me. On the day of the election they nominated Dr Imad, my friend, who was already the chief resident. He was very popular, everybody liked him. Nobody ran against him and he was elected unanimously.

We opened the nominations for the vice-chief resident and I shocked everyone when I didn't nominate myself. Even the doctors who hated me were stunned. I told them that I'd taken on the responsibility of the hospital when nobody was there and had worked very hard over the previous two months. I'd done my share and now that everything had settled down, I believed it was time for the new doctors to take responsibility as I withdrew from everything.

Three people were elected. One of them, Tariq, was one of the highly religious people who were unhappy about me. On the first day after the election, Tariq came to me and asked me for the keys to the medical supplies. I asked him why, and he said that he had it from a reliable source that I was selling the medications.

I was very upset at the accusation and asked Tariq to go with me to the director of the hospital. On the way there we came across some guards who asked me why I was upset. When I told them that Tariq had accused me of stealing medical supplies and selling them, they were enraged and one of the guards put his gun to Tariq's head and said that he would kill him. These were people who liked and respected me for my honesty. I ate with them, looked after them and they answered to me, so they were seriously angry about the slur on my reputation. I eventually managed to calm the guards down and drag Tariq away.

I introduced Tariq to the director and told him that Tariq was the new vice chief resident. I also told him what Tariq had accused me of, asking him to set up an official investigation. The director and I had had our differences in the past, but he told Tariq that he would have accepted an accusation against himself but never against me. He was angry, told Tariq that he trusted me, and that there would not be an investigation. The director then kicked Tariq out of his office.

As things happen, Tariq and I became good friends later down the track.

Perilous times on site

One day I was called to emergency because a man and his seventeen-year-old son were using a crane to loot the university. The guards and the looter exchanged gunfire resulting in the son being shot and killed. The son's body was brought into emergency for his death to be certified. It was a terribly sad time.

The father was sitting silently in a chair in shock. I couldn't talk to him and I couldn't blame anyone. It was a stupid, unnecessary death. The father shouldn't have been looting and the guards could have simply shot into the air. It was such a waste.

Another day, the guards called me at five o'clock in the afternoon. Imad and I went to a checkpoint to find that a male nurse, red-faced with embarrassment, had been detained. He'd been stopped with bag full of drugs stolen from the hospital. He'd collected the drugs on his shifts by writing on patients' charts that the drugs had been administered and then stashed them to sell outside later.

The guards could easily have killed him. That's how volatile, excited and undisciplined they were as it was such a lawless time. Personally, I did not particularly like the nurse and had never been impressed with his work, but I couldn't leave him to the mercy of those crazed guards.

I told them that we had to all sit down and discuss what had happened. I asked them to bring me three pens and three sheets of paper, and began to slowly examine everything in the bag.

As I wrote down a description of each item, the tension began to ease slightly. On I plodded, painstakingly writing for fifteen minutes, as Imad wondered what the hell I was up to. The guards looked on without saying a word or questioning my actions. After filling the first sheet of paper, I copied everything onto a second sheet, and then onto the third. Gradually, the guards' energy levels subsided until they were reasonably calm.

Next, I asked for the nurse's personal details and asked him to sign a certificate stating that he'd stolen the drugs with the intention of selling them. Imad and I added our names and signatures and then had all the guards do the same. This seemed to take forever, but by the end of it, everything was reasonably cordial again.

I told the guards that one copy of the pages was to go to Imad, the Chief Resident, who would give it to the director of the hospital the next morning. I told them the director should start an internal investigation and punish the guy according to hospital policies. I then gave a copy to the nurse, with the last copy going to the guards. I told them that their copy was in case nothing came of the investigation, they would have evidence.

When I then told the guards that we were going to let the nurse go free, they argued against it. I informed them that we were taking the drugs back to the pharmacy and that an investigation would be started the next day, and they finally seemed reasonably happy.

The very next morning at eight o'clock, Imad and I went to the director, but he already knew about the nurse. The guards had told him because they thought that I would try to cover for the nurse and that I was stealing with him. I gave the details to the director and thought the matter was over. I was wrong.

A new force

The leader of the transitional government of Iraq, an American diplomat named Paul Bremer, decided that anyone of a certain position in the Ba'ath Party would be fired from their job. The mother of one of the guards, a member of the Ba'ath Party, was fired from her job at the hospital because of this.

At the same time, the hospital received communication from the Americans that anyone who had been paid a salary in the month before the fall of Saddam would not be fired and would continue to receive a salary. There were two contradictory laws in operation.

The guards discovered that the nurse who had been caught stealing drugs was back working at the hospital. Going to the Americans, they told them about the guard's mother and the nurse, both of whom should be able to return to work. The American troops were very upset about it all, wanting to know how such a thing could happen. It was then that I found them arguing fiercely with Dr Tariq, the person appointed to my old position.

I heard one of the Americans shouting, so I intervened. I told the Americans that we had no authority to fire anyone in the hospital. One soldier asked why not, and I told him that the coalition-appointed governor made the rule that anyone who'd been working at the hospital before the war could not be fired.

The American then asked why the lady was fired and I told him that she shouldn't have been fired, that it was against the law, and we should bring her back. I told him we needed a new law and a new standard.

When the American asked who could make the new standard, I said that once we had a new government we would have someone who could make a new standard and a new law. The Americans laughed. 'Yes,' they agreed. 'That's a democracy. Iraqis should become a democracy and make their own laws rather than rely on the Americans.' I totally agreed with him.

The American told everyone to leave, then pointed to me and asked me to go with him. Tariq was fine with that because the Americans had been so upset and now, with my intervention, they'd calmed down. The American told me that he could see that I was a very good person and that I understood what was going on. He then said that the volunteer guards were very good people who had a very good cause, but his superiors didn't like them because they were regarded as militia and they were linked to a religious figure. He said that his superiors were going to kick the guards out of the hospital and bring in other people. I told him I understood that. In fact, three months after that talk, the guards were released from their duties and a new team was brought in from an organisation linked to the Health Minister. They used formal recruitment methods to select the team to protect the infrastructure.

After the soldier had spoken with me, I went back to Tariq at the doctors' administration. He was laughing and he asked me how I did it. 'The Americans like you, the guards like you, the director of the hospital likes you and everybody else likes you.' I told him that I wasn't doing anything. People simply liked that with me, they knew what I stood for. Thinking back, I believe I was popular because my agenda was very clear. My priority was the patients and the hospital: how the hospital should continue running, and how the patients should get treatment there.

The hospital director's agenda was linked to the previous regime and he struggled to keep his position. The guards also had their own agenda. They volunteered to protect the hospital, but their masters tried to take Saddam's place. They not only controlled the hospital, but they also controlled the electricity in Iraq. And the Americans had their own agenda – they were running the country.

I was in the middle. I had nothing to gain and I was not trying to steal anything. I often found answers that were logical and acceptable. I always came up with something and could convince people to agree. I found solutions when things were very tense and difficult. I was always calm and quiet and could pacify other people. I was very composed because I was always very clear about what I wanted.

I didn't have anything to prove. I was there, and I thought I should improve things.

The American soldiers

In the hospital, things had settled down reasonably well. People were working and accepted my authority. One day, an hour before sunset, the guards told me that an American soldier wanted to talk to me.

A Caucasian lieutenant who looked around twenty-seven years old was waiting for me outside the main gate. I can't remember his name, but he informed me that his men, about fifteen of them, and three tanks were being based at the hospital to protect us. I noticed that he was the only light-skinned one in the platoon, the others being Latino, African American, Italian and Asian.

I took him inside the hospital grounds along the big drive where he was surprised to see our guards with weapons. He asked who was in charge, and I explained that the hospital was well protected by our volunteers, that we had no problems and didn't need his soldiers.

The lieutenant was impressed with the arrangement but said that he'd been ordered to protect us, so there was no choice in the matter.

I explained our system of checking in with the guards on entering and leaving and how most people were happy with it because everyone was Iraqi. I suggested that if they had to stay, then they should remain out the front of the hospital where they'd be more efficient and leave our people to look after the back where it was dark and covered with trees and shrubs. That way there would be no misunderstandings and accidental shootings. I was also concerned that if the Americans were attacked, we would somehow be held responsible.

The lieutenant agreed and was also happy when I suggested that our guards stayed alongside his soldiers. With our guards speaking the local language there would be better communication when visitors and staff were checked for weapons or stolen goods.

I could also foresee a problem at night when our guards would be patrolling and would encounter the Americans. How would the Americans know our guys were friends and not attackers? I suggested that we were supplied with green glow sticks to light up when approaching the Americans at night.

The lieutenant and I chatted while we sorted out other details and I introduced him to the guards. He told me that he had a bachelor's degree in physics and was engaged just one week before being deployed. That was the only personal contact I had with the lieutenant. However, with his men, it was a very different story.

That same night, I returned to the doctors' accommodation to find Errol from Pennsylvania visiting. At thirty-three, he was the oldest in the platoon, very friendly and a non-stop talker. It might have been stress that kept him going, but he told us that he didn't know his father until he was twenty-eight even though he lived in the same street.

When he told us that it was quite common for Americans not to know their fathers, we were amazed, and though we thought it was hilarious, we began to appreciate our cultural differences.

Errol shared his very nice Camel cigarettes with us and was happy to take some of our poor quality Iraqi smokes.

We talked about many things, and a few days later he brought seven of his fellow soldiers to my room. Luckily I had a lot of space, because they all decided to play dominos.

The idea of dominos is to keep your tiles hidden from the other players and calculate which numbers are remaining in the other players' hands. It's all about strategy and memory.

Not for my colleagues. Intending to win, they shared what they had with each other in Arabic. It was hilarious. Even cheating, they still could not beat the Americans. We've no idea how those guys did it, but they always won. They were a lot smarter than we initially took them to be.

At night we'd often go to the front gate and chat with the guards and soldiers. One of the buildings was the out-patients' clinic which had a flat roof. Some of us went up there with the soldiers and they showed us their infrared scope. It was amazing. We could see clearly in the dark for 400 metres: people walking and driving vehicles.

An African American, a huge guy called Brian, talked with me a great deal about the war. We became friends, and he explained how he and his friends felt. Showing me a fist, he pointed at it and said, 'This is Bush.' Pointing at his other fist, he said, 'This is Saddam.' He then banged his fists together and said, 'They're the ones fighting, not us. Not you and I, the American people and the Iraqi people.' Brian told me that he was unhappy having to fight this war and that was why he was reaching out to me.

In fact, we had few opinions about the war. We just wanted the Americans to get rid of Saddam. Concerned only about getting our work done, we had no idea about the future of the country.

The more we talked with the soldiers, the more we saw that they were no different to us. They were just regular people like us – a different culture, sure – but we laughed and clowned around the same. They were also impressed that we'd talk to them because in the States many doctors were standoffish and too arrogant to talk to ordinary people. We, on the other hand, were more humble and easy

The American soldiers

going. And we had no political opinions that could cause conflicts.

One night, around 11 o'clock, Errol from Pennsylvania came to see me alone. 'Dr Issam, I feel unwell,' he told me. Suffering from a fever and diarrhoea, he'd left his platoon without saying anything to anyone. 'I just I wanna sleep somewhere,' he said.

I knew that the platoon had to sleep in a tank without a bed, so I took him to my room and gave him mine. Placing his weapon on the floor, he stripped down to his underwear, took off his boots and lay down. I covered him with a blanket, and he fell instantly asleep.

My room was close to the TV and main hall, so I went there to watch TV and talk to the other doctors. I didn't mention Errol.

At 3 o'clock we were still watching TV when Errol appeared in his underwear on his way to the toilet. Everyone sat up straight. 'What's going on?' they asked. Pretending I hadn't noticed, I said nothing. They must have had all sorts of strange thoughts.

In the morning Errol woke up around 7 o'clock feeling much better. He got dressed, picked up his weapon and went back outside without anyone knowing any better.

We have an Islamic name – Ibn Al Sabeel – that refers to a traveller who is lost or stuck, away from family, or has no money. This person is one of the eight people under Islamic law that we are obliged to donate to, including the poor, the orphaned, the unemployed, people working for no money and the traveller in need of help.

I didn't think of Errol as an invader. He was a human being, away from his family, and sick. Not only that, he trusted me.

It wasn't all roses, for sure. One day Errol and some of his platoon were sitting with us and our guards at the gates having a chat. He started telling us about an incident during the war when an armed Iraqi soldier walked towards the platoon. He was shouting in Arabic but wasn't understood, so the American kept yelling, 'Stop! Drop your weapon and put your hands in the air!' The Iraqi wouldn't stop, so the American, becoming more afraid the closer he got, shot him dead.

Unfortunately, Errol laughed when he told us that. And at that, the entire group of people went silent. I looked around and saw grim, pale and stunned faces.

The man didn't deserve to die. He wasn't pointing his weapon at anyone. His crime was not understanding a language completely foreign to him.

As Errol realised the terrible insensitivity of his words and began to apologise, we sat in shocked silence, thinking about the man's wife and children. He was someone who did not wish to be in Saddam's army and made to go to war. And we saw him as a person, whereas Errol regarded him as a soldier on the other side – a foe to be eliminated.

Without another word, we all got up and left Errol to his thoughts.

Errol would eventually understand however, that people in the US saw Iraqis only through the American sniper's telescopic lens. We were all evil and determined to kill all Americans in the name of Allah, and yet there was nothing further from the truth.

I was at home one day when one of the American soldiers was brought unconscious into the coronary care unit. My colleagues couldn't determine what was wrong with him and then a senior American doctor, Gonzales, came to examine him. Apparently, he was suffering from a drug overdose, and Dr Gonzales immediately evacuated him to the American base.

Later, we found out that one of our doctors, a real joker, had been supplying anti-psychosis pills to the American soldiers for recreational use. The pills had some interesting side-effects where the troops would laugh inappropriately in front of the lieutenant or fail to wear their helmets or carry their weapons when on parade. Of course, the lieutenant went ballistic.

Naturally the Americans thought they had a major drug problem and were concerned. Suddenly, they withdrew the troops from the hospital without even a goodbye.

I had no idea where the Americans were or why until a week or so later when one of the ambulance drivers delivered a note and some shaving lotion. The note and gift were from Brian, who explained that they'd been relocated to guard a detention centre in the city, and could I come by sometime and say hello?

A few days later, I was in the ambulance and asked the driver to stop at the centre. Brian came out to see me and told me that they'd been redeployed because of an internal investigation regarding the drug use. He also informed me that they'd all agreed to admit to having the drugs but not to disclose the name of the doctor concerned to keep him out of trouble.

I later discovered that this particular doctor – who incidentally is a very good friend of mine – put a tablet in my tea. He was very disappointed when I just went to sleep.

It may sound bad, but we were all so very young and mischievous then. We were in constant danger and under pressure and being naughty was a way of blowing off steam. The soldiers also loved him. He was always clowning around and making everyone laugh. It's why they were determined to protect him.

The new section of the hospital

No one except the director of the hospital was permitted to go to the new block at our hospital where Saddam's equipment had been transferred. I had the key but I never used it.

One Friday afternoon (Friday was part of the weekend), the guards came to me and said that they thought there were terrorists in the new part of the hospital. Before the end of the war, Syrians had volunteered to help Saddam and there were about four thousand of them in Iraq. The guards told me that armed Syrian terrorists were in the hospital and that the director had let them in. I knew that was utterly false. I believed they just wanted to check on what equipment was in the hospital, choosing a weekend when the director was absent and I was the only one around. I didn't trust them an inch.

I told them to give me fifteen minutes because I couldn't open the door without a committee otherwise I'd be in trouble with the director. I needed the head of the engineers and three or four doctors who were older than me to give the incursion a sense of legality.

Arriving at the new block, I could feel tension building among the guards. One of them used the butt of his AK-47 to break a window and then fired a shot because he was upset that I'd prevented them from storming into the building immediately.

Adil, one of the doctors (who is now a general surgeon in Iraq) told us he was resigning from the committee and leaving. In the meantime, I managed to calm the others down by telling them I would open the door if the guard took his finger off the trigger of his weapon.

Adil returned, later telling me it was because he felt sorry for me. We entered the building and saw all the new equipment, including three new pistols in one room. The guards said they wanted to take them; I told them they could because guns were of no use to the hospital. But they were to leave the equipment alone.

We found a very nice operating theatre where the guards found a brand-new stethoscope and said it was for me. I knew what they were up to. If I took the stethoscope, they could take other things. Telling them that I couldn't take anything for personal use because it was the hospital's equipment, they kept insisting I accept it. Finally, I told the guards that the stethoscope would be put in the doctors' accommodation so that if a doctor turned up without a stethoscope they could borrow it. One of the doctors, who is a surgeon now, took the stethoscope and never returned it.

The guards found Viagra and one asked if he could take it. I told him he could but he'd be punished by the other guards. He then argued that no patients would need it. Again, I told him that he could take it, but that God would punish him (which meant he was not allowed).

They always pretended to be religious so I was talking their language. Believing that God was the observer and if they stole anything God would punish them, they returned the Viagra.

Unable to remove anything and without finding any terrorists, I had the committee sign a statement that nothing had been taken except the weapons and the stethoscope. However, when I handed the statement to the director, he was upset having already discovered the broken window. It took a while but I explained that I'd been manoeuvred into opening the hospital wing up and that's why I'd formed an emergency committee of responsible and respected staff members.

That strategy had, in fact, prevented a large-scale looting of equipment and drugs, and at minimal cost. Relieved, the director told me that the hospital was in debt to me ... again.

The newer section of the hospital was not used until a new director was elected. At that time, I created a committee of eleven with people from all the departments and the director. We went from room to room and recorded all the equipment in each room. The committee signed the list of the equipment that I then handed to the director. One of the interesting things on the list was the dental records of Saddam's son.

Corruption in the hospital

In fact, everything was stolen later by the new hospital management. They were all completely corrupt. I'd kept everything safe, I handed it over intact to them, and then it was gone. Luckily, I always made copies of things like handovers and kept one copy for myself. This was widely known so nobody could accuse me of corruption.

We thought everything wrong with Iraq was linked to Saddam. Things like the corruption, the unfairness and the injustice. I believed that every single person in Iraq was suffering from Saddam's rule and thought that we had learned from experience and would now do the opposite.

Six months down the track, the new Iraqi government was in place; the Americans had handed over to the Iraqis. The Ministry of Health and the Shi'a had brought in their own director, put him in power to oversee the hospital. At that stage I was no longer on the scene.

The first decision the new director made was to fire thirteen doctors just because they were Sunni, transferring them to different hospitals. It was out-and-out discrimination.

It was then that I realised that things were the same as when Saddam was in power. All the corruption had sprouted up again. It was incredibly disappointing after feeling the hope of a new era. The first two months after the war was the best time at the hospital in terms of fairness, justice and everyone having rights.

And then it collapsed. Perhaps I was naïve, thinking that people would have learned that corruption was a cancer.

All the people around me, the doctors and my friends, remembered me and what I had done. I was not alone. I had been brave enough to take on the responsibility, but they all helped me. Whatever I asked them to do, they did. They were very loyal. Under Saddam, there was only ever one way. The doctors had different ideological and political backgrounds than me, but despite these differences they united to support me. They had their own ways of thinking but they too were proud of that golden two-month period after the war.

*

After moving away from hospital responsibilities, I started to focus on my study and my work. In the first year of my training to be a specialist, it became more than just doing my basic duties of going to see patients. I was spending more time in the hospital and the doctors' accommodation studying. I aimed to be a specialist of internal medicine, a four-year training period.

Despite everything happening on the political scene, exams were still running. My university was the first one to start back after the war because it wasn't damaged. Our study took place in the hospital and the Iraqi board who supervised the training declared that the exams were still on.

We had the exam in October, six months after the war's end. Unfortunately, I failed that exam. It was a tough one and I was disappointed that I failed, because I did study for it. Only four or five passed out of the thirteen in that first year. But I continued to train in the hospital and repeated the exam twice before I passed.

Despite my work and study, I had more time to see my family.

Explosions at the Holy Shrine

The hospital is in the same town as the site where one of the grandsons of the prophet was buried – a very holy shrine and one that I was really fond of. Every year, on one particular day, many Shi'a celebrated at the site where the grandson was killed in a battle. Usually one to two million would come to visit, and in March 2004 I volunteered to be at the hospital tent at the holy shrine.

Some take part in a ritual where they injure themselves on the head with a knife. It's a very old tradition. Causing a lot of blood, they're trying to emulate the grandson. There's a lot of debate about whether that part of the ritual should remain because it's cultural rather than religious.

There can be thousands of injuries, some of them severe. I volunteered with others from the hospital to provide aid and to be there for those who wanted to donate blood rather than engage in head-hitting. All the roads were closed to traffic for this event and were filled with sad and crying people in mourning.

I volunteered for both morning and afternoon; one of the guys, Ebaa, who is now a plastic surgeon in France, asked if he could go with me. Ebaa was Sunni, not Shi'a, and he wanted to watch the ritual. He came with me, both of us wearing our white coats in front of the holy shrine.

At that time, the Americans participated for the first time by protecting the ceremony, setting up a checkpoint in one area while local volunteers secured the other. With many bombs being detonated recently, there was a fear that somebody would attack the ceremony.

At 11 o'clock there were two explosions. They were about 150 to 200 metres away from me. The first explosion was in the shrine close to where I was. Everyone instinctively dropped down to escape except me – I was standing, looking at the shrine and shouting, 'No, no, don't destroy it.'

I was so attached to the Holy Shrine. Over a thousand years ago, the Imam Al-Khadim was buried there. He spent his last 15 years in prison as a political prisoner. He supported the poor and worked for justice for all people. The Shrine represents all the principles of justice and equality that I believe in. Seeing it destroyed in front of my eyes was like destroying a vital part of my soul.

My friend pulled my hand and I went down as another bomb went off inside the shrine. When the explosions finished, we all stood as an American tank arrived. Just then, an Iraqi guy with a loud-hailer said, 'These Americans did this.' Everyone there, thousands upon thousands of people, attacked the American tank with shoes and stones: the Americans had to escape.

The injured were brought to the tent. We had a surgeon with us, a military doctor before the war, along with a few nursing staff, and some doctors. We soon found that many victims were burnt; we gave first aid before putting them into ambulances or cars to be transferred to hospital.

Working very fast, we were finished after ten minutes. The surgeon with us looked at me, bowed and said, 'Issam, it's now time for a tactical withdrawal.'

Asking him what that was, he whipped off his white coat, rolled it up and held it in his hand. Suddenly, he was no longer a doctor. Asking me to go with him, we walked through an ancient part of the town for about forty-five minutes. By the time we arrived at the hospital, although we could smell the smokiness from the injured, the doctors at the hospital had done well; they'd dealt with the influx and sent people to theatres or off to wards, so there was nothing left for us to do.

Back in the doctors' accommodation, I saw that two of my friends were extremely distressed, having never seen anything as shocking as this before.

Dr Riaydh showed me a piece of green cloth called a Rayat Al Abbas[2], something usually placed around the neck. The green represents the flag of the ancestor of the prophet and when people wear it, it's like a blessing. He told me that an injured man he'd been treating had taken the cloth from around his neck and given it to Dr Riaydh. He was deeply touched by that.

More than one hundred people died that day, and another five hundred were injured – not just in the explosions at holy shrine near the hospital, but at another holy shrine in Karbala, about one hundred kilometres south of Baghdad. About five million people gathered to celebrate there.

Nine explosions happened at exactly the same time as the two explosions in my hometown. They were the start of explosions that targeted my town and the villages. Within the next few years there were more and more explosions. We started to get used to them.

Whenever there was an explosion all the doctors at the hospital would go to the emergency room, including surgeons and doctors who were not a part of the emergency room teams. They would be ready to help the injured. Usually there were not enough beds available so people would be treated on the floor.

---

2. Rayat Al Abbas means 'flag of Abbas'. Hussein was the grandson of the prophet Mohammed and Abbas was his brother. Hussein was killed in the Karbala battle in Iraq 1, 350 years ago. Abbas was holding the green flag after all Hussein's family and followers were killed. Hussein, Abbas and the women were the only ones who remained. Abbas went in to fight and he lost both his hands but didn't leave the flag. Abbas was killed in the end. People believe the green flag of Abbas will bring blessings.

Iran

In June 2004, I was going to the mosque close to home to pray when a man from my home town asked me if I wanted to go to Iran to visit a holy shrine. In Iran there is a holy shrine for one of the twelve imams we believe in, and it is a great honour for Shi'a people to visit. There are seven holy shrines in Iraq, one in Iran and the remaining used to be in Saudi Arabia, however they were destroyed over 90 years ago.

When I asked how much it would cost, he told me that ten days' travel and accommodation cost less than a hundred dollars. No passport was required because we could obtain a temporary passport from the Iran government. This would be the first time that I left Iraq.

My friend, who had travelled before, told me that once I left the border of Iraq into Iran we would get a different type of wind. Iraq was very dry, so I looked forward to that. We went by land, travelling with old ladies and only five men. Arriving at the border, we were checked by people from the coalition forces because there was no Iraqi government. I'm unsure of the coalition forces' nationalities but they weren't American.

In the first moment I left my country there was the wind. It was beautiful – so refreshing and gentle. Travelling by road for thirty-two hours, we went through lovely towns connected by excellent roads. It was an interesting and replenishing trip.

Going there as a simple visitor, I had no intentions of living there but enjoyed the quietude. We could go out at any time of night without encountering trouble – a nice change from Iraq.

Although the language is different, Iran is predominantly Shi'a. In Iraq, when people come to visit the holy shrine in my town we regard them as blessed people and we try to help them. In Iran, we were visitors to the holy shrine and, as our religion dictates, people should have helped us. Two things happened that contradicted that.

One day, I was in the market wanting to buy a Coke from a shop. Once the shopkeeper realised I was Iraqi, he said he didn't have any. I thought perhaps he'd had friends or family killed in the Iran–Iraq war.

The second thing was that I saw a guy in a wheelchair in the markets. His legs had been amputated. The markets were very old and the land not flat, so it was hard for him to negotiate the markets easily. Just to be helpful, I put my hand on the wheelchair and started pushing it. I pushed him for about two hundred metres before he wanted to stop to buy something. He hadn't turned to look at me at this stage.

When I started to talk with the shopkeeper in Arabic, the guy in the wheelchair heard me, turned and saw me and went crazy. He refused to let me push him again. It turned out that he was a victim of the Iran–Iraq war.

It was sad to see, but the wealthier or more comfortably-off Iranians certainly didn't like Iraqis. They didn't care that we were visiting the shrine and had no qualms about not helping us as they should have.

After midnight, there were different markets. Very poor people would come and put their things to sell on the ground – they didn't have shops. When I went to buy some souvenirs from a lady, she kissed me when she realised I was from my town with a holy shrine. She was related to the Imam, the religious figure from where I came from. The poor people were different – it was like they had religion inside them. They had the emotion and empathy of our religion. The wealthy didn't care.

*

Back in Baghdad, things worsened. Between 2004 and 2005 there were many explosions, and the Sunni people as well as some Shi'a turned against the Americans. With American troops inside the towns, there were constant troubles.

Car bombs targeted the areas of mainly poor people or Shi'a, and many of the injured were coming to our hospital. Many friends left the country and other doctors were finding jobs outside medicine. We were paid about $120 a month and the hours were long. A job in the call centre of a mobile phone company, would pay $1,000 a month, so some doctors went to work there. Others would work in a humanitarian organisation: one of my friends, Hamad, became a manager at Mercy Hands. The organisation received financial support from America for various projects and my friend would be sent on conferences about refugees or internally displaced people. Other doctors went to work for the Red Cross.

With the war against Saddam over, the insurgents were now fighting the Americans, and politicians started targeting the police and Iraqi army. There was no rest. I stayed in the hospital working because that's where I felt most needed.

Saddam was captured and executed. I was at the hospital that day, and with my colleagues, stayed up all night waiting for the news of his death. The execution was at five o'clock in the morning. Because I'd been up all night, I slept in until about ten o'clock and then heard that there'd been three car bombs in my mainly Shi'a home town. The main road in my town was burnt without a single shop left, and 150 people died.

They were unstable times. Early one public holiday morning, we were woken by someone who'd entered the doctors' accommodation and was yelling out wildly for 'the sons of bitches doctors'. We were told that he wanted to attack us because there were people waiting in the emergency department but only a few doctors there – most had left for the holiday celebrations. We quickly closed our door, but as we didn't have a key, we put a chair up against the door and hid under the bed. We laugh at that now, but it was a dangerous incident.

When he finally left, we went down to the emergency department where things had already been sorted out.

*

On our first day back from Iran the new Iraqi government took over.

The coalition government formed a local council composed of twenty-five people from the Iraqi opposition – they were all people who had been in opposition to Saddam. They chose from all different types of people – Sunni, Shi'a etc. The Americans knew them all beforehand. Every month one of the twenty-five would be the head of the council. The prime minister was someone who was very close to the Americans. The council lasted for about six months and then they changed to another government.

Eventually an election was held in January 2005; finally there was a stable government.

Marriages

In Iraq, we have arranged marriages. Approaching twenty-nine, I thought maybe it was time for me to get married. If a man wants to marry, he becomes responsible for providing a home, furnishings and anywhere between five and twenty thousand dollars' worth of gold. Of course, a junior doctor in my position couldn't afford that.

A man lives with his parents until he's married; we don't leave home after reaching adulthood because nobody can afford a house. After marriage he then lives with one of the parents: houses in Iraq are large to accommodate this. For example, my mother's house has eight bedrooms.

In 2005, I noticed a girl working in the hospital laboratory. She was very pretty, tall and very light-skinned. She wore a hijab and appeared to be a modest and respectable person. I'd seen her from time to time, but I'd never actually spoken to her because she was a conservative person. Talking or dating were prohibited and any communication had to be through third parties or in secret.

I mentioned to one of the doctors in the laboratory that I was interested in the girl, and asked if someone could talk to her because I was thinking of an arranged marriage. He volunteered to do that and, finding that she was very positive, suggested that I talk to her family.

She gave the doctor her parents' address in Karbala, a hundred kilometres south of Baghdad. He gave the family my details – which family I came from and where I lived. The normal process was that her parents could then ask around about me and see if my family and I had a good reputation.

A little later, she told the doctor that her parents were happy to see my family to talk about an engagement, but there was a problem. The highway to Karbala was called Death Road. Any Shi'a travelling on that road would likely be killed by terrorists fighting against Shi'a people and attacking civilians and their vehicles.

I was unhappy about endangering my family and uncles on that road. Wanting to marry was one thing but having my family die because of it was quite another. Deciding to go to Karbala myself, I asked Ahmed, one of my friends from there, if I could go with him when he visited his family.

Although our trip along Death Road went without incident, the girl's family were upset that I arrived without my family. They had a house in Baghdad they went to from time to time, so we arranged another meeting when they could meet my family.

A couple of weeks later, Hakeem, Saleem and my mother went to the girl's Baghdad house and that was the start of our engagement. But a day after that, the girl told me that she didn't want to marry me after all. 'Look at my face!' she said. 'One of my eyes is artificial. I had it removed after a childhood medical condition and it's better that you find someone else to marry.' I told her that it would be unethical to do such a thing. 'What if I had an accident after we were married, and I lost an arm?' I asked. 'Would you leave me then?' At that she seemed happy and I thought everything would then proceed smoothly.

Three weeks later, her father called me and said that the engagement could not continue. I asked him for the reason and, despite my objections, he passed the phone to his wife. She unpleasantly informed me that it was because I had no money. When I said that I was a doctor and the money would eventually come, she told me that she had no other girls to marry off and that was it.

I heard from my friend in the lab that the girl married an uneducated guy from Baghdad three weeks later. Older than her by ten years, he was also wealthy. A month later she was divorced over money issues.

They didn't care about me as a person, or of my achievements and ethics. They just cared about money. The girl was a good girl and I don't think she was of the same mind as them; she had no say, nor did her father. The mother controlled everything.

Theoretically, Iraqi tradition is that the man has the word and women have none. A man's word is his honour and can't be broken, but a woman can say anything and not be brought to task over it the same way a man can. If I make a mistake, compensation can be claimed from me by law because my word is the word of a man. If a woman does the same, compensation cannot be claimed because she is a woman.

In the marriage process, money and religion are the major factors. Nobody cares about you as a person, your morals, your ethics, or the love you may feel for someone.

Civil war

During 2005 and 2006 it was basically civil war in Iraq. The Sunni let off a bomb in one of Iraq's five holy shrines and blew it up. As a result, the Shi'a people started to kill Sunnis. Going into the streets, they either kidnapped or outright killed any Sunni they found.

The Shi'a identified people's religions by asking their names. My family had lived in my town for forty years, so I knew which neighbours were Shi'a and which were Sunni – that was general knowledge. Shi'a people from my town started attacking Sunni and killed several hundred of them. With the remaining Sunni driven out, the town became purely Shi'a.

In the Sunni areas they began killing Shi'as. There was no law. The police were mainly Shi'a, so they wouldn't protect the Sunni people. Militia and itinerant people without proper authority created checkpoints to check IDs. If you were the wrong religion in an area, it would mean death.

The very next town to us was Sunni so my home was on the frontline. Sunni would kill anyone walking in the main road, so I stayed at the hospital and went out less and less. Many of the medical students would stay as well and my room became like a refugee camp.

I would also have some doctors who were not part of the hospital stay with me. Because of my past strength over the issues we'd faced, the hospital's administration had some respect for me and didn't bother me over it, so I was able to protect a few people that way.

One guy, Zaid, was Sunni. His father's name was Ali which is also a Shi'a name. His father was killed because the Sunni believed that he was a Shi'a.

We brought Zaid to our hospital which was all Shi'a, with a militia who would kill him. I asked my friends and some students to call him Sayyid Zaid. Sayyid Zaid means that he belongs to the prophet and was Shi'a. Sayyid literally means 'mister' but in Iraq the word is a title for anyone who is a direct descendant from the prophet Mohammed. The last time we celebrated Zaid's birthday, our wish for him was that he would escape to another country. Eventually he did just that and now lives in Sweden.

Wisam, my friend who worked in a call centre, became afraid because a friend of his there was killed by the militia, simply because they regarded anyone working in the call centre as collaborating with America. One day, a man came to the doctors' accommodation asking about Wisam. He happened to not be there, so a doctor asked who the man was. 'The Barber,' he replied. The Barber was a savage and notorious killer who would cut off his victims' heads. He had come to kill Wisam.

I had been sharing my room with Wisam and Hamad. I had no security on my door, there was no key for the lock, so Hamad, who worked for the humanitarian organisation, decided that he wasn't coming back to stay at the hospital. Being the manager of the organisation, he was able to convert a room there into somewhere to sleep.

When Wisam found somewhere else to stay for a while, I became afraid that the Barber would return. He knew which room his target slept in, so I slept somewhere else in the hospital for a while. A few months later, we saw on the news that the Barber had been imprisoned and we breathed a little easier.

The times were hard, and I became depressed. Seeing so many bad things around me for so long was getting to me. I was afraid for my brothers because anyone could go out and not come back. Afraid to answer any phone calls from my family, I expected to be told any day that one of my brothers had been killed.

One day I was shocked to get a call from one of my brothers at five o'clock in the morning. It turned out that one of my neighbour's sons was injured and in need of help. From time to time, I found people from my town in emergency, shot by snipers. I became more and more anxious for my family.

In 2005, I was at the hospital when Hakeem called me asking me to come home. My family was escaping the next day to the south of Iraq where our tribe and my surviving sister, Eklass, were living. He didn't give me more information.

I packed my bags with clothes and twelve medical books. I was preparing for my final exam and, despite the odd situation, my studies remained a priority.

When I arrived home, Hakeem told me that he'd found a death threat note at our door, stating that we'd be killed. There was some confusion because the person the note was actually intended for lived locally – it wasn't for us. Our family did not want to take any chances.

Hakeem went to the main mosque and spoke to the Imam. He requested the Imam to use the loud speaker to inform the town that our family were victims of Saddam as we lost our brother just few years ago. We hoped the killers would hear that.

Next morning, we left our house and belongings and escaped to the south.

At that time, my oldest brother Saleem was in Syria with his family for a month's holiday. Hearing the news, he decided to stay in Syria for the time being.

I stayed down south for two days with my sister but I couldn't stand it there any longer. Things in the south were bad – there was no sewage system, no paved roads, and it was a very dusty place. I went for a walk and was unable to stop thinking about my work and study. Telling my family that I'd stay at the hospital, I returned to Baghdad.

Eventually, a month or so later, my family were called by neighbours and told that they could come back because nobody would touch them, and they'd be protected.

When Saleem heard what was happening, he decided not to return to Iraq with his wife and two children. Applying for work in Syria, he found a job as a lecturer. Later, he went to Egypt for a year before his visa expired and they then moved to Kurdistan.

*

Christians were also targeted in their towns. Two towns in particular suffered –New Baghdad, a small town with a Christian majority, and Al-Dorah, a town near a big oil factory which is predominantly Christian. Many of the Sunni who lived in those towns participated in the terrorist attacks, clearing the towns of Christians. As many were killed, kidnapped or threatened, the remainder left their town and the number of Christians went from fifty thousand to less than a thousand.

In my hospital was a student called Numan who was Christian. A very serious person with white skin and a thick moustache, he was very quiet although his friends and colleagues were very naughty boys, laughing and joking all the time. Numan had strict rules and followed them carefully, going to his well-arranged bed early.

Living in a predominantly Sunni area, he spent all his time with us at the hospital. But one day he left the hospital and was caught at a checkpoint by outlaw militia who were looking to kill any Sunnis. There was also a police car there.

When they asked Numan for his name and ID, he asked them why he should give it to them. These guys had guns and they'd kill for nothing. But he stood his ground and demanded to see their IDs first. Laughing, they asked him to repeat what he said. Numan told them that he'd give them his ID if they were policemen. But they weren't, so he wouldn't.

Nobody would normally talk to them like that. They were violent criminals and we just prayed to God when we encountered them that they would let us go. In the end, they called the police over. The problem was that the police were corrupt and supported the militia instead of targeting them.

Numan showed the police his ID. His surname was Aleya, a Christian name. They asked Numan if he was Christian, he told them he was. They then said that he was 'on their head', which was a form of respect. They said that they liked their Christian brothers, and if Numan had said he was Christian from the start, they wouldn't have annoyed him. They let him go.

When Numan came back to the hospital and told us the story, we all laughed. He was certainly a brave man. We had a naughty bravado but weren't brave like him. He was a serious person who followed the rules, and, for him, those were that if someone asked you for your ID you first checked who the person was before complying. Only Numan would do that.

*

The militia captured Dr Odey, a famous ear, nose and throat surgeon, in the front of the hospital. He fought them, but they forced him into the boot of a car, drove off and his body was never found. The same thing happened to another prominent surgeon not long after.

One day, I was sitting in the cafeteria with Anas, one of my Sunni friends, and five others who were doctors and students. Anas had recently finished a master's degree in pacemaker physiology and had scored eight points in EILTS, an English exam set by Cambridge University. To migrate to Australia or the UK this exam must be passed; it involves reading, writing, speaking, and listening. Nine points are full marks, five are required for a visa application, and six point five will allow study for a masters' degree in Australia. To practise medicine in Australia requires seven marks. With Anas's eight, he told me that he was planning to apply for immigration to Australia.

As we chatted, one of the guys received a call from his family. They told him that there were militiamen around the hospital, grabbing people. All of us were using the hospital accommodation, except Anas. He was driving back home because he chose not to use the hospital accommodation. I told Anas to stay with me in my room and not go home until the next day. We warned him that if the militiamen caught him he'd be in trouble.

Later I was told that Anas had left in spite of our warnings. The following day his aunt, who worked at the university, came to us and asked if anyone had seen Anas. It sounded very much like the militiamen had taken him.

The militiamen then called Anas's father, an engineer and head of the School of Engineering at the university and demanded that he pay $30,000 to get his son back. He raised the money and then drove off to meet the militiamen. Despite following the kidnappers' demands, neither Anas nor his father or their cars were ever seen again.

I am pictured second from left. My late friend Dr Anas is second from the right.

It was so frustrating: we were well aware that sort of thing could happen and that's why I had pleaded with Anas to stay at the hospital. Within an hour, he'd decided to leave without telling us. I really don't know why. Perhaps he felt that the danger was less than we thought, or couldn't believe that anything that bad would happen.

*

When Saddam took power, he executed many of the Shi'a in the party, accusing them of being linked to Hafez al-Assad, the Syrian president. Assad – the father of the present-day Syrian president Bashar al-Assad – was also a member of the Ba'ath party which was controlling both Iraq and Syria. There were talks about unifying Iraq and Syria and making them one country.

The Ba'ath party's aim is to combine all Arab-speaking countries into one. Saddam didn't support the idea because he wanted to be the undisputed leader, and accused any Ba'ath member who was close to Syria of conspiring against him.

My friend Khalid was born in Iraq in 1978. His father was in Saddam's camp and a very high figure in the Ba'ath party even though he was Shi'a. There is a famous video where Saddam calls out the names of the suspected party members and has them executed. Khalid's father was one of those named, but managed to escape with his family to Syria.

Saddam took their house and everything they owned when they left. Khalid lived in Syria until 2004. He studied medicine there and then came to our hospital after the war when Saddam's regime collapsed. While the family was living in Syria, his mother died of cancer, and that made the remainder of his family decide to return to Iraq. When they returned to Iraq, they were able to reclaim their house.

Because Khalid grew up in Syria, where there was less violence compared to Iraq, he was quite different to us. He was quiet and very kind. We were hardened in Iraq because of the constant violence in our lives. It was difficult to have manners and we were tough – we needed to be. Khalid was so different, and everyone noticed it.

Everybody felt ashamed of their lack of empathy when they were with Khalid. All the doctors in the hospital appreciated his soft nature and good manners, and he was genuinely a kind person – not at all like the rest of us. Our culture of violence and aggressive behaviour is endemic. When people tried to bully or mock Khalid, he'd just laugh and walk away. We really learnt from him.

Khalid and I became very good friends. I was still in training and preparing for the final exam in 2006 and was studying with him. We would read and question each other – a good way to study. Khalid decided to go back to Syria to do the MRCP (Membership of the Royal College of Physicians) at an exam centre in Syria. I was interested as well so we studied and applied to take it.

Khalid sat the exam first and passed the first part of three. I sat for it about five months later and passed the first part as well. Khalid's family did not use their house in Syria because of the violence in 2005 and because it was in a Sunni area. An uncle and two of his sisters went there only on Saturdays to meet with Khalid who was studying there.

On one Saturday, Khalid met with his sisters and his uncle as usual when a gunman entered the house and shot and killed Khalid, his uncle and one of his sisters. The remaining sister received a severe head wound and was blinded. Unaware that her siblings and uncle were dead, she was flown to Iran for surgery.

I had finished seeing patients and was going to the doctors' accommodation after having something to eat in the cafeteria when I met my close Sunni friend Ahmed on the stairs. He was weeping and when he saw me he started sobbing loudly. I couldn't understand what he was saying. He wasn't the sort of person to cry like that at all. He then managed to tell me that Khalid was dead.

I took Ahmed to my room and got him to sit down so he could tell me what had happened. I needed to support him, so I couldn't cry or let my emotions take over. I felt terrible, but I had to calm Ahmed down. It was later that I allowed myself to feel the deep sadness.

The entire hospital was devastated. It was one of our worst days. One friend, Mohammed, who was also Sunni and was particularly fond of Khalid, just wept day and night. Another friend gone – it was too much.

Khalid was the most genuine person. In all my twenty-three years of study and work, I'd never met anyone quite like him. Nobody can take his place in my heart. We lost so many doctors and friends during those difficult times, yet his death affected more people than any other. His ethics and principles were strong and steady and in the two years that I knew him well, I never heard him swear or say anything detrimental about another person. People tried to push him to reveal his bad side, but he just didn't have one. He left a huge hole in so many lives.

My late friend Khalid.

Ahmed and Khalid had shared a room at the doctors' accommodation. After Khalid's death, Ahmed kept Khalid's PlayStation and a wall poster. Ahmed printed a photo of Khalid and hung that in the room as well. When I was returned to Iraq in 2014, Khalid's things were still in the room. Nobody had touched any of them.

Ahmed was Sunni and Khalid was a typical Shi'a, descended from the prophets and very religious. Yet Ahmed loved Khalid – it was beyond religion. Ahmed told me he had never met someone like Khalid with such character. That was how Khalid affected us

– crossing religious boundaries and getting into another's heart.

Khalid had really wanted to become a member of the Royal College of Physicians UK, so I knew I had to do it in his honour. I was already qualified but to go that extra step meant a lot to me.

*

In those days, I was deeply and constantly worried about my family. At any time, I could have received a call that one of my brothers had been killed or kidnapped. Two of my brothers were working as taxi drivers. The militia moved their checkpoints around so if you went down the wrong street and ran into them, they could take you or kill you.

Our house was on the border of Sunni and Shi'a dominated areas, which meant my brother was forced to carry a weapon. Townspeople had come to our house and told my family that one of my brothers should protect the community at night. My family didn't like weapons, but my brother had to go out every night to protect the town. It was his duty.

At the time, we had an AK-47 at home; it had been there since before the war although we'd never used it. Every house had weapons: it was abnormal not to have them. My brother's watch on the town didn't last long, just a month or two, and then things started to get better.

The last time I saw the AK-47 was on my 2014 visit. The gun had been thrown into the roof space, was rusty and no longer working. I asked Hakeem about no longer having weapons and he said that they left it to God. They're very trusting. There are no locks on the doors, and Hakeem said that if anyone wanted to steal from them, what would they take? They had nothing.

My family also never had a problem with the Sunni. At that time, it was common to have 'mixed' marriages. Nobody would ask if you were Sunni or Shi'a. Now it is different and there is division in the community. My family decided not to be affiliated with any political party. The parties are always fighting for power and my family likes to be independent from that.

We are a very religious family in a way that we can see God all the time.

I went through more than most people go through – I witnessed people killing each other and doing their worst. God was with me all the time. I never got hurt by anyone, despite all the danger. I believe that whenever you don't hurt any other person and you have a good heart, God will be there to protect you.

Despite all the hardships of living in Iraq, my family were good with others. People were stealing, killing and doing bad things: many people were criminals or corrupt. There was also the day-to-day pressure of life itself. My family didn't go with the wind or with the ocean waves: they stood apart from the majority of people doing bad things and didn't follow. I believe that if you have been good, when you die then you are comfortable.

With our culture and religious background, we think about life after death. We believe that we will be questioned about anything we did in our life – good things and bad. My family did good things despite the difficult living conditions and community they lived in, one that encouraged violence and corruption. Even with those things around them, they did not become corrupt. They remained kind and good. If God exists, and there is an afterlife, they will be answering the questions without any problems compared to criminals.

While I was studying for my exams, my salary was about $200 per month. I didn't have a computer, so I talked to Hamad, who worked for the humanitarian organisation. As he had a good salary, we decided to buy a computer together. We paid $200 each and bought a desktop. It was good timing because I started to get all the questions for the previous MRCP exams and used them to study, study, study. I also played some music on the computer while I studied. All my friends played computer games on theirs but all I used ours for was study.

I contacted one of my friends, Tim, who had left Iraq earlier and was then living in England. He generously paid my website joining fees for the British Medical Journal in preparation for the MRCP exam. I started to sort out the questions and in 2007 I went to Syria to do the MRCP.

I passed. And I honoured my promise to Khalid.

Shi'a bridge

In 2006, I had also passed the theory exam in Iraq to become a specialist. I still had to sit the clinical exam in Medical City, in the centre of Baghdad. There was one big problem – getting to Medical City, I had to pass over a bridge called Shi'a Bridge. It was called Shi'a Bridge because it was in a Sunni area and any Shi'a who crossed the bridge would likely be killed.

For two days, I was anxious about going to the exam. I wasn't concerned about the test; I was afraid of getting killed. It wasn't just me, there were five of us who were Shi'a intending to go to those exams. I was so distressed and anxious that my throat became painful and my voice changed.

At seven on the morning of the exam, we were all wearing suits and holding our bags ready to go. We had one very religious doctor, Dr Moayed, who told us we should leave the hospital by different doors. I asked him why.

He was thinking of a story about Joseph and Jacob the prophet. Jacob the prophet had a son in Egypt. He sent eleven of his twelve sons to Egypt and told them to go into the city through different doorways so people would not see them together. It was to avoid harm. That's how Moayed was thinking. He thought that if we all went together we would be noticed, but if everyone went by themselves no one would particularly pay attention to us. So, we went through different doors, met at the front gate and caught a taxi.

When we left the hospital, there was silence in the taxi. We were very apprehensive and scared. I am sure all of us were watching the streets and thinking about the bridge, not the exam. We reached the edge of the Shi'a town and the taxi was driving over the bridge. It was early in the morning. The sun started shining. While I don't recall my colleagues' faces, I can remember their breathing patterns. Their breathing was shallow and no one was able to say a word. We were scanning the sides of the streets and looking ahead for any armed men. There were none. Leaving the bridge and approaching the hospital our breathing relaxed and we started to talk about the exam. It was reality now: we would sit the exam. We arrived safely.

In the clinical exam, the first case I saw was an old man with heart failure. He had both his legs amputated above the knee, so he was wheelchair bound. I had forty-five minutes to gather his information before the examiner would come. As I started, the Sunni militia fired nine missiles at the hospital. The Sunni area was very close to the Shi'a-run hospital and very close to the Ministry of Health, which was also run by the Shi'a.

I continued taking the patient's history, while in the background I could see everyone running and leaving. My patient couldn't leave because of his amputations. After the attack the examiners returned and pretended nothing had happened. I was asked a lot of questions, but I didn't pass.

After we finished, we met up with Moayed: now we had to get home. Deciding not to go from the front door, we went out the back where the hospital met the river. Suddenly a sniper began shooting from across the river. Moayed told us not to look back and just run. Someone had been shot behind us. Running, we found a taxi and jumped in. Managing to get back to the hospital safely, we were very relieved.

It wasn't an exam at all. It was a horror movie.

Working at the clinic

Finishing my four years without passing the exam meant that I didn't have a lot of duties, so I studied a lot. Every Saturday morning, I stayed with my consultant at the internal medicine clinic and then went back to my studies.

We were meant to have thirteen professors or lecturers for specialty training. For each couple of professors, there was supposed to be a team and we were to train as part of each team. Because of the civil war most of the professors wouldn't attend. Only three consultants or professors continued to come to the hospital and they had to train around forty doctors.

I was fortunate. I was attached to Professor Hashim, the head of the unit, who happened to live in the same town as me. He was always at the hospital – he never stopped working and I attended the outpatient clinic with him.

The first patient that came to us had the Rayat Al Abbas (the green flag) around his neck. I questioned him about his chest pains as the consultant watched on. He was suffering recurring chest pain and was not on any medication.

When I asked him about his scarf, the patient told me that three days earlier three of his sons were going by car to the Shi'a festival at the holy shrine in the south of Baghdad. The Sunni attacked the car with bombs and they were all killed. I asked the consultant how we could control this patient's suffering. It wasn't a medical condition – it was just too much sadness.

Another time there was an orthopaedic surgeon, a very kind doctor. I didn't know him personally but when he worked with us I always watched him. You could tell a good doctor very easily because of their manners and their ethics. He brought his mother to the clinic. He was working in an outpatients' orthopaedic clinic and he asked me if I would look after his mother because he had to go back to his clinic.

His name was Omar, a Sunni name. He belonged to a tribe called Meshhadani who lived in my hometown. Most of the people from that tribe were killed or displaced. As he was Sunni and was practising in our predominantly Shi'a hospital, there was a very high chance that he would be killed. We saw his mother who also suffered with chest pain. When I started to take her history, I asked her if she was worried about her son, Omar. She started crying. I told my consultant that it was obvious what the cause of the pain was, and that medication would not help.

My hospital in Baghdad.

Treating two patients in a row – one a Shi'a man who had lost his three sons, the other a Sunni mother whose son was at risk of being killed – was heartbreaking, particularly as this was a training clinic. It was very hard at that time. We would go to the clinic to escape from reality but would constantly find people who were suffering.

The Endeavour Scholarship

When I went home one day in 2006, my brother told me about our neighbour, Dr Juma'a. He was old, very obese, and had been in the military as a doctor at the time of Saddam. When Saddam was gone, there were no military doctors, so he joined the Ministry of Health. A diabetic, he wasn't looking after himself very well even though he was a doctor. My impression was that he was not a smart man.

My brother told me that every night Dr Juma'a would come to our house and ask for me. Although I didn't know him, that evening I knocked on his door and I asked him how I could help.

Juma'a brought out an eight-page application for an Australian scholarship called the Endeavour Scholarship. He told me that his brother in Jordan had sent the papers to him and had told Juma'a to apply for the scholarship.

Juma'a couldn't read English, so he was asking me to translate and fill in the application for him. As I read and translated, I saw that the scholarship required the applicant to have an English score of 6.5. He couldn't read a word of English. He also had to have acceptance from an Australian university or research centre to go and work with them. The other requirements were that the applicant had to submit three referee reports and a research proposal. I looked at him and he told me not to worry about it. I left him with a bit of a smile on my face.

The next morning, a Saturday, I was in the clinic with my consultant. In the middle of the clinic my consultant printed out an email and gave it to me. It was from an Iraqi, an engineer and a professor at Monash University in Australia. He'd met my consultant before the war at a conference Saddam had organised in Iraq for all the Iraqi people overseas who had tertiary qualifications. Saddam had wanted them to advise and co-operate with Iraq about education.

The email to my consultant said that the Australian Government was giving six research scholarships to high-achieving individuals in Iraq. They would pay AU$25,000 to cover living costs and research expenses for six months. The name of the scholarship was the Endeavour Scholarship.

I thought, 'Oh my God, that's the same scholarship as the one Juma'a was applying for.' My consultant asked me to take the email to my colleagues in training and tell them about it. When I told them about it and that the details were online, they started to laugh at me. They asked why Australia would give Iraqis scholarships. Nobody was interested in applying.

On my way home, I thought to myself that Juma'a and the consultant had come to me with the same scholarship. It must be a sign from God that I should apply for the scholarship because nothing happens without a reason. I thought if God wanted me to apply for the scholarship then God would give it to me and I would leave the country.

At that time, many doctors were leaving and going to Jordan. They stayed there for two or three years, suffering, until they could escape to America or other countries. I didn't have enough money to go to Jordan so the scholarship was my only option.

There was not a single person who didn't laugh at me. Even my family laughed at me. Only Hamad and Ali Amer helped me, because they believed in me.

As my computer didn't have internet access, I risked the 500-metre journey down the road from the hospital to an internet café – many people had been kidnapped and killed in the area. I found the scholarship website and downloaded the application form and everything that related to it to a USB flash drive over a two-hour period. I was relieved to be back in the hospital.

I read about the three types of scholarship. The first was for six months of post-doctoral research. The second was for six months of a master's degree – six months in Iraq and six months in Australia as an exchange student. That wasn't for me. The third was for a master's degree or PhD in Australia. For the masters, you needed an English qualification, which I didn't have. For the post-doctoral I only needed a letter from my supervisor to say I had enough English proficiency to perform post-doctoral research.

I chose the post-doctoral option, which required conditional approval from an Australian institution – a university or hospital or research centre. That was the hard part. I also needed a research proposal.

The second time I used the internet café, I realised how difficult it would be to continue my application online there – it was very expensive and also very dangerous. So, I decided to bring the internet to my accommodation. I talked with the guys who ran the internet café and they told me I needed to put a very large tower above the hospital to get the signal. I did that with the help of friends, and I started to get onto the internet while I was in my room.

I didn't have a CV nor did I have email. I asked my genius friend Hamad to help me. I needed to send an email to the university to get approval; I had to put together a CV. I was working on the application every night. I had five weeks to submit my application.

I knew nothing about Australia. In Year Seven Geography we studied the map of Australia, and we had one chapter about

Australia where it talked about the climate. But they didn't talk about the people or the life there.

The only thing I knew: I could draw a map of Australia!

*

Now I needed to send emails to universities. I surfed the net and found a very helpful website called the Directory of Australian Universities. I then looked at every university and every medical school. I looked at the buildings; I looked at what they had and what their tuition fees were, I looked up who to contact. But I was looking blindly. I didn't get information about Melbourne, Sydney or Brisbane. I simply selected five universities whose tuition fees were low. I thought that if I was given $25,000 I would have to pay fees and I needed to survive.

I started to send emails to the international students' section. I didn't have a research proposal: I just told them that I was about to finish my specialist training. I thought that once I had finished my training in 2006 I would be able to do post-doctoral research because my degree as a specialist is regarded as a PhD in Iraq. I told them I was interested in doing research and I planned to do it with the Endeavour Scholarship. I also told them that I needed conditional approval and I was interested in diabetes research.

I was checking the emails every five minutes at night after I had sent out my requests. The good thing about Australia is that people will reply to you even if the response is negative. In Iraq if the answer is negative, they don't reply to you. Every day I got replies – sorry, sorry, sorry. Then one day I got an email from a lecturer at Charles Sturt University. The university is located at Albury Wodonga, which is on the border of Victoria and New South Wales. The lecturer, Herbert, told me he was interested in helping me.

We chatted every day via email. I sent him my CV, and after two weeks he asked me to send him my application. On the application was my story. I wrote about my childhood and how my father died when I was a child. How I had just started to know about death and then my sister died. How it became very hard for me because I learned that death would take our loved ones. I told him that I then decided to be in the medical profession just to help defeat death. I explained how we didn't have internal investigation capabilities in Iraq and that we depended on physical examination to get a diagnosis. The purpose of my research was to focus on improving my skills in that aspect.

He emailed me back and told me I had had a phenomenal life, that my story touched him. He sent me the application with a research proposal that he wrote for me. That was very important because I didn't know what sort of research proposal to submit; I didn't know what was available in Australia. He wrote it and, not surprisingly, his language was very good. He sent me a letter of acceptance that he would be my supervisor and a letter from the head of the school.

I had met all the conditions. I went to my consultant and asked him to sign the paper stating that I had good English skills. I told him it was for the scholarship in Australia that he had told me about. My consultant signed the paperwork and didn't even ask about it.

Many times, when I was at the accommodation using the computer and internet for the application, my friends would come to my room and laugh at me, except for Hamad and Ali Amer who were helping me. My other friends were pessimistic. They told me about a guy who applied for a scholarship in Germany. They said he was very smart and he'd ranked two in his class, but someone else was chosen.

I finished the application and sent it in August 2006. The results would be released in January 2007. By that time, I had taken the exam for the specialist training and had failed. I was disappointed because if I wanted to do the post-doctoral research, I needed the degree. In January 2007 I was in the library at the university, which by that time had the internet. On checking my emails, I discovered one from Julie Bishop. At the time she was the Minister for Education and Training in the Australian government, and she was overseeing the Endeavour Scholarship.

The email, signed by Ms Bishop, said they were delighted to inform me that I had been granted the scholarship. It was an amazing moment! In the same email, they asked if I would accept the offer. Of course, I would accept! I was so happy.

Later, I was sent a link to apply for a visa and told I could apply online to the Australian embassy in Jordan as the Australian embassy in Iraq didn't issue visas. It is very hard to get a visa if you are from Iraq, but I had the letter from the Australian Minister of

Education. The embassy in Jordan asked for evidence that I was still employed in Iraq, which I was going to find to be an almost impossible task.

*

I went to the hospital and told them I was applying for a visa to Australia and asked them to write a simple letter saying I was still working at the hospital. After a few days, the director of the hospital, who was one of our consultants, did it for me. I also needed a summary of service. If a doctor was travelling overseas, any hospital would ask for evidence of the first year of training, an internship.

No Iraqi hospital would provide it to any Iraqi doctor.

In Iraq, doctors are subjected to unfair laws. We are not allowed to get any document that proves that we are doctors, whether a diploma or any simple document like a paper stating that we are still employed. These laws were inherited from the Saddam era to stop doctors from leaving the country.

The hospital told me that the director had signed off on the paperwork but that I should get approval from the main branch of the Minister of Health, which was about two kilometres from the hospital. They refused to give the signed documents to me; instead they sent them by post to the branch. After a few days, I risked going to the branch so that I could pick up the signed documents. It was the end of the month and I only had 4,000 Iraqi dinar, which was about three dollars. That was the only money I had because I was waiting for my salary.

I arrived at the branch and asked the man doing my papers if I could apply for six months leave, because I was afraid if I went to Australia and then came back they wouldn't give me back my job. I told him that I hadn't had any leave in the seven years I had been working at the hospital. He refused. He then took the papers to the administration director. The director wore a suit with no tie. That meant he was very religious: in the Shi'a religion, some believe that the tie represents the cross of Jesus. They don't want to be associated with that in any way – which is narrow minded because it was just a tie and has nothing to do with Jesus at all.

When I asked him if I could get a signature, he told me I could but it would cost four million dinars, which is AU$4,000. For a pharmacist it was two million dinars. I asked if it was a legal thing. He said no, and that I should work it out. He meant it was under the table. He wanted me to bribe him for the document saying I was still working in the hospital. And he was making a show of being religious by not wearing a tie.

It is very clear in Islam and the holy Quran that if anyone takes or gives a bribe, they go to hell, no matter what they did in their life. The man had the position at the branch because he belonged to the Islamist party which ran the new government. I showed him the four thousand dinars that I had and I told him that was all I had. I told him I was not giving him any money and I asked him for the papers.

He gave them to me – but without his signature.

As soon as I left I looked at the documents. One of them was the summary of service and the director of the hospital had signed it! That was the document that the hospital wouldn't give me. They'd said I had to get it signed by the branch of the Minister of Health. I didn't need that signature because the director had already signed it. It was valid and Australia would accept it. I never forgot that. I was so happy. A friend helped me to translate all the documents and send them to the embassy in Jordan.

After four months of study, I sat the exam again in May but unfortunately, I didn't pass. I was disappointed because my plan was to sit the exams in May and then to travel in June. I was told I should go to Jordan to pick up the visa or send someone else to do it, so I would have the visa stamp for my passport. Luckily, I had a lot of friends in Jordan. My friend Ali Amer was working for a French humanitarian organisation and flew regularly to Jordan. His role was to take Iraqi children with heart conditions there, and from there the children were taken to France to have their operation.

I sent my passport with Ali Amer when he next travelled with the children. The passport was taken to the embassy and I got the visa stamp. When I got my passport back I took it to my family and they said it was not real. They thought it was a fake and that someone had tried to steal my money. They were very simple people.

In the meantime, I contacted the organisation that was running the scholarship to tell them that I didn't think I could come because I hadn't passed my exam and couldn't do post-doctoral research.

My friends fought me over my telling the organisation, arguing that I shouldn't have told them. But I was very honest and wanted to stay that way. A lady from the organisation emailed me to ask if

I still wanted to come to Australia. I told her that of course I did. She said they would accept the research as part of my training, but she just needed a letter from my supervisor saying that they were happy for me to do it as part of my degree. I went to my consultant. He gave his permission. I was so excited to get the signed paper I ran back to the hospital accommodation. I scanned and emailed it the same night.

The Endeavour Scholarship organisation accepted the signed paper from my consultant. I had my visa in my passport.

In one of my visits home, I showed my family the passport with the visa stamp. Hakeem said it was a fake, and he didn't believe that Australia would give me a visa. My mother believed that the people who contacted me wanted to take money from me. I told them no, it was all real. Then they told me how my cousin who lived in Dubai visited my family and explained to them about scams. My family didn't really believe that I would be going away. They were probably in denial.

I decided to go via Jordan and on to Australia from there, and had one of my friends book my ticket.

I was about to leave when I suffered a severe anxiety attack. I was so scared – I thought Australia was a black hole. Imagine leaving Iraq, where it was so dangerous and thinking Australia was frightening! The day before the flight I could not eat or drink and I collapsed. It was all psychological. Cancelling the flight, I went home.

My friend Hamad had to postpone the flight for me for another week. Then the same thing happened again in the lead-up to the rescheduled flight – I had another attack of anxiety. The doctors put me on an IV fluid. I just could not do anything and I cancelled the second flight – that was how afraid I was to leave. On my third attempt my friends would not talk to me; they were really upset. They wouldn't book the flight and they didn't come to say goodbye to me. I booked the flight and my friends said if they saw me the next day they would hit me.

I paid a friend of mine to take me to the airport because of the kidnapping risk. I had borrowed $3,300 from my brother Hakeem and I'd also borrowed $800 from Hamad to buy a laptop. Many people were waiting for the plane. Terrified, I couldn't eat or drink anything. Eventually, arriving in Amman, the capital of Jordan, I thought I was finally on my way.

The Endeavour Scholarship

Oh, but no! At the airport I was taken to a room and someone from Jordanian intelligence asked me what I was doing. I told him about the scholarship from Australia and had all the emails from the Minister printed out for him to see. I said I was staying in Jordan briefly before leaving for Australia.

Many Iraqis go to Jordan and then apply for refugee status. He asked me how much money I had. At that stage I had only $2,000 after paying for my tickets. He didn't believe I was going to Australia with only $2,000 and accused me of entering Jordan to stay. I was denied entry and put in detention at the airport.

I was to be sent back to Iraq the next day.

*

In Jordanian detention I was put in a room with eleven other Iraqi men. There was another room with all women. One of them was an old lady who had eye problems and had come to Jordan for an operation. They didn't allow her to stay.

I was sitting on the floor in the room with the other men. I couldn't eat or drink and I was unable to breathe from the psychological tension. There were no chairs in such a small room.

There was no lunch or dinner for anyone. We were told that we would be sent back to Baghdad. The next morning, we were put on a plane back to Baghdad but, approaching the city, the flight couldn't land because of a dust storm. We flew around for forty-five minutes before the airline decided to return us to Jordan.

We were put back into detention and given something to eat. That afternoon around

This picture was taken in July 2007 when I was detained by Jordanian authorities at Amman Airport.

two o'clock they said they were sending three of us (myself and two others) back to Iraq. This time we were put in first class because there were no other seats available. That was quite nice because we got a lot of orange juice and were treated well. Then we were back in Baghdad. I arrived home to my family and everyone laughed at me.

The following day I went to the hospital and they asked why I was back and what I had done this time.

On the way to Jordan the second time my anxiety had increased, but when I went back to Baghdad my anxiety left. I think part of the anxiety was leaving my family, and going to somewhere I didn't know. In a way, in the end I was forced to go to Australia because everybody around me wanted to escape Iraq and my friends were pressuring hard. When I thought I would just try for the scholarship, I really hadn't seen myself going anywhere. But then I got accepted. Everybody was pushing me, telling me I earned the scholarship and to just go.

Yet, I was afraid. When I returned to Baghdad I was more comfortable. The anxiety had gone and I was laughing and I started eating. I'd been afraid of the unknown. My mother asked me why I had become cowardly and I told her I was just human.

*

After my Jordan experience I decided to go via Syria. At that time they allowed Iraqis to enter and there were flights onwards to Australia.

The day that I left for Syria was 25 August, 2007. Hakeem and my mother were at the front door. I was trying to say goodbye and I was close to tears. My mother and Hakeem said together, 'Don't cry. Turn your face and go,' and I did. I held back my tears, turned my face away, and not looking back, I left.

Fortunately I had friends in Syria; Odaey, who was a Christian and a pharmacist, and Asham, the brother of my friend Tim, who is now a doctor in Vienna. Asham would hang out with us at medical school and after graduation. We had a very good relationship. I arrived in Damascus and immediately took a taxi from the airport. At that time my friends were living in a refugee camp.

Al-Yarmuk is a refugee camp for Palestinians. During the war in 1967, many Palestinians were sent there, and subsequently built houses within the camp. Some of them have lived there for thirty or forty years. Odaey was at the refugee camp waiting for a visa to Australia. His parents and his only sister had already left Syria and they had applied for him. It took ages. He'd been waiting for a visa for two or three years. They had sold everything in Iraq so there was no other place for him to live.

Asham was also waiting in Syria for a visa, but his was for Austria, as his aunt and all his extended family were living there. Money-wise, things were not very good for them – Odaey and Asham lived in a basement. They called it the humidity club. Why? Because the basement was an underground room made of concrete, with no light, no windows, a bathroom but no kitchen. It was so hot and humid. They had no choice because it was the only place available that they could afford. So, I joined the club.

Asham sometimes did crazy things and would often fight with the landlord. When I moved in, we visited the landlord. I told him I was going to Australia and that I was a doctor. The landlord started to be respectful to my friends. He must have decided that they were very educated and not bad people after all.

On my first day in Syria, I went to book a flight to Australia. The flight was booked for September 2007, so I was to stay with Odaey and Asham for three weeks. Their lives had become boring so they were glad I was there. When I was with them there was a lot of laughing and we hung out together a lot. We did a lot of crazy things. I remember one day there was a wedding and there was music, so Asham and I jumped in the middle of it and danced. Asham was a little bit impulsive; it was fantastic and we didn't care.

Syria is a beautiful country, so beautiful that Odaey and I decided we would go to Australia and get citizenship, and then come back to live in Syria. People were so educated there – it was different from Iraq. At ten o'clock at night there were groups of girls and boys who would go and hang around out outside. They were honest and approachable and formed proper relationships with each other, whereas in Iraq people would be cheating and lying.

Education was valued in Syria. The British Council conducted English courses, something we didn't have in Iraq. The people were affable and the girls were very beautiful. Prices were very cheap compared to Iraq, they had cinemas, and the natural environment was lovely. Syria was a very peaceful place. I enjoyed my three weeks there – it was like a holiday.

Before I left Iraq, I was told that on arriving at the airport in Syria, you should just give everybody four dollars and they will do everything very fast. I put four dollars in Syrian currency in my passport and gave it to the officer. The officer immediately signed me through and said nothing. The Syrian government was very welcoming towards Arabs. Syria's Ba'ath party's goal is to unite all Arab countries into one, so they welcome all Arabs. They had a different approach compared to other countries. Jordan, on the other hand, practised discrimination.

Those three weeks in Syria had normalised things for me a bit. The relaxation was strange yet good, and I laughed and went out a lot. In Iraq, I couldn't go out and had become depressed over time. It was excellent therapy for my bruised spirit and I began to feel more comfortable about getting on a plane to Australia.

Part Three:

Australia

An important meeting

When I was in Baghdad applying for the visa to Australia, I was asked to do a medical test. I had to go to a specific hospital to see a specialist who did the medicals. A girl who had also applied for a visa to Australia was doing the same tests. We were together for every stage of the tests but we didn't speak as we didn't know each other. At the end of the test, she finished before me and left. I departed five minutes later and noticed her standing at the hospital doorway looking at me. Initially, I didn't talk to her because in Iraq you just don't do that. As I walked away, I saw her face change to an expression of disappointment and realised that maybe she was waiting for me.

Going back to her, I said 'Hi.' She seemed happy to be approached so we started to talk. She told me her name was Dunia and she was applying for an Australian visa to be a carer for her brother who'd had an accident. His name was Issam. After telling her my story, we exchanged phone numbers and promised to call each other regularly to see how our visa applications had gone.

Dunia gave me her brother's mobile number and told me he'd help me. Before I boarded in Syria I let him know that my flight was landing in Melbourne at 4 am; he offered to come and meet me and take me to his house. There were no excuses for me not to get on that flight now.

After forty-eight hours of travelling and stopovers, I arrived in Melbourne on 19 September 2007. At the airport, customs singled me out and I was stuck there for an hour. They questioned me, wanting to know what I was doing and examined all my papers – the scholarship documents and my letter from the Minister. They asked me where I was going to be living and if I'd booked a hotel; I told them no, but that someone was coming to pick me up. They asked me how I knew him, and I said that I knew his sister in Iraq. They were laughing at me and at my handwritten passport as if I'd made it all up.

In the end, they asked me for Issam's phone number, which I gave them. When they called him, he told them that he was right there at the airport waiting for me. Then they released me

– Australia allowed me in. After the cost of the ticket and other expenses I was left with only $300.

I met Sam (short for Issam) and he knew who I was immediately. Years later he told me that I stood out because of my clothes and how desperately tired I looked. Sam had been in the war when Iraq invaded Kuwait in 1991. When America won the war, he escaped to Saudi Arabia, and stayed there in a refugee camp for two years until he was accepted as a refugee by Australia. He arrived in Perth in Western Australia, and then came east to Victoria.

Sam took me to his very clean house where he lived alone. He had a business painting and rendering houses. He left me to sleep, but because I was very afraid he would steal my remaining money, I hid it. That's how ingrained I was with distrust of Iraqis.

I slept for twenty-four hours and when I woke up Sam had made me something to eat. My anxiety was back and I couldn't eat a thing. I slept again. The second day, Sam decided not to go to work until late but to stay with me. Again, due to the anxiety, I couldn't eat. Sam had to buy paint for his business, so he took me with him in his car. I remember looking out at the streets and noticing they were all very, very pleasant. He took me to beautiful St Kilda, where he usually drank his coffee at 5 am every day at a French café before going to work, and introduced me to his friend, the owner.

I had only American dollars, so I told Sam that I needed to change it. Sam told me later that he was shocked that I'd come to Australia with so little money. He thought I had at least $10,000. I also opened a bank account at that time but, unfortunately, it wouldn't be activated for five days.

Leaving me at an internet café, Sam went off to work and told me that he would pick me up in the afternoon. He suggested I go to the beach, but I first sent an email to the organisation managing the scholarship with my bank details because they wouldn't transfer any money until I had the account. They told me that they'd initially send me $10,000 – five for the airfares and five for six month's accommodation costs. I also emailed my supervisor to let him know that I'd arrived.

I couldn't go to the university at Albury until I had that money, so I was waiting and checking for it every day. Sam was worried and wasn't sure that I was getting it, but in spite of that, he looked after me.

An important meeting

I stayed with Sam for a week, and we'd go to St Kilda and have a coffee every day. Sam would then go to work while I enjoyed the beach and wandering around. It was amazing. His house was in the Sunshine area near a creek and a beautiful park I'd walk to. He was so kind and helped me very much in that first week.

Calling my supervisor, I told him that once I received the money I would move to Albury. The university had two weeks off so it was good timing.

In the meantime, Sam taught me many things about the law and customs of Australia that were so different to Iraq; things like the issues of sexual harassment and manners. One day, Sam invited me for lunch at a restaurant. A lady came over and asked me if I wanted a drink. I said no to her; just 'no' without a 'thank you'. Sam turned to me and explained that in Australia that it wasn't good manners to do that. He said that everyone was a human being and we should say 'No, thank you.' That was an important lesson because we didn't have that in Iraq.

I learnt so much about those differences during that week. I was really lucky to have Sam. I didn't know him but he gave me accommodation, he took me around, helped me to open a bank account, and showed me some very lovely places.

I was disappointed to find out a year after my visa was granted that Dunia, Sam's sister who had given me his phone number, had been denied a visa.

*

After five days, I had the funds. It was such a good feeling. Sam was delighted and told me that he would take me to Albury, telling me that if I was moving there I would need furniture and household items. He took me to a second-hand shop where I bought plates, cutlery, a mattress for $20, and a few chairs (I still have some of those plates). My purchases weren't even $200, and included a TV.

Sam put everything in his utility and we left for Albury. Before I left Iraq, I'd checked out all the accommodation there, going to real estate websites to understand how far places were from the university and their costs, and then printing it all out.

The trip to Albury took five hours, including stopping at a winery for breakfast. When we arrived at Albury, Sam took me to a real estate agency where the agent told me there was a unit available for $100 a week but that I needed a referee. Sam offered to be my referee, I signed the contract, and we all went off to the unit. The agent told me that the electricity wouldn't be connected until the following Monday. I laughed. 'That's fine,' I said. 'I'm from Iraq.' He and I later became friends.

It took only a few minutes to put my mattress and TV on the floor and my plates away. It was time to say goodbye to Sam who was going straight back to Melbourne. He'd been brilliant; we're still good friends and see each other regularly. It was sad that Dunia couldn't get a visa and had to continue to live in Iraq.

After Sam left, I decided to walk around the town and see the university. Sam had told me to use the six months at Albury as rehab. Although he was laughing, he was serious when he said that I was suffering from depression, and as Albury was a country town it would be good for me there.

Walking to Charles Sturt University, I was surprised to find that all the buildings were houses. Later, the university moved to Thurgoona and was in a unique building – environmentally friendly, and probably the only university in the world to generate its own electricity, collect rainwater, and have environmentally friendly toilets. But when I was there, it was just old houses surrounding a square. In the centre was a cafeteria, a laboratory, and the lecture halls. Disappointed, I didn't go inside. I'd flown thousands of miles to come to this small university. Why had I left Iraq with its extensive university buildings – for this? Ultimately, I'd be proved very wrong. The standards of teaching were very high and miles better than in Iraq. Perhaps that initial disappointment was also a reflection of my state of mind, loneliness and exhaustion.

Settling in to Australia

On the Monday after arriving in Albury, I went to the university. It was all very quiet as there were still two weeks left of the holidays. I found Cheryl, a nurse working in administration. She contacted Herbert, my supervisor, who took me through the university and decided that I'd start working in research the following week.

Herbert had a diabetes clinic where patients would come for research purposes. He is not a doctor of medicine but has a science PhD. Testing of each volunteer patient took an hour; I checked their eyes, urine, sugars and heart. Collecting the data with Cheryl helping me, I would see patients from eight-thirty in the morning until five in the afternoon.

Part of the test involved taking blood from the volunteers. As I was taking blood from one lady, she told me she felt funny. 'Why?' I asked, thinking she wanted to laugh. Just then, as I noticed her pallor, Cheryl came in and realised my patient was fainting. After I'd elevated her legs and removed the needle from her arm, Cheryl explained that 'funny' meant dizzy. This was my first encounter with Australian slang and I was so embarrassed. Later, I bought a book about Australian slang. It was very useful.

I also worked with Bev, our technician, and everyone was very kind. Sometimes podiatry students would come to the clinic, and Herbert would ask me to give them some tutoring. I was delighted to do that, discovering how inclusive the Australians are. People would constantly ask me how I was doing and how I was settling in.

I was invited to a Christmas party although I wasn't Christian. I met Santa Claus and everyone asked me what foods I couldn't eat (pork) and made sure those needs were respected. It was an indication of the good manners practised in Australia compared to Iraqi bluntness.

I started to explore my neighbourhood and meet people. I was living in a complex of many single-bedroom units, and met a neighbour, Paryanta, a very special character. A Sri Lankan Buddhist and an experienced immigrant, he was friendly and helpful, so we became friends. Paryanta kindly helped me improve my spoken English, and watching him, I learned more of my new environment. He worked hard in a cheese factory by day and washed dishes in a restaurant at night.

Paryanta's plan was to save money, obtain permanent residence, marry and buy a house. It was a solid dream. To save, firstly, he'd cook enough rice for two weeks, put it in containers and use only one every day. Secondly, he'd go to the Sunday markets and buy four kilos of apples for $4.00. He'd seldom buy food from supermarkets and criticised me for doing that. He'd only go on Tuesdays when the price of bread was low.

One day he came to my unit and saw that I had pink tissues. He told me that the pink tissues were very expensive and I should only buy the white ones. I was shocked that I'd been wasting my money and went to check. The difference between white and pink was two cents. That was hilarious.

English and medical exams

Back in Iraq, my friends had told me to sit the Australian Medical Council and English proficiency tests, just in case I was able to get a job and stay. Arriving in Australia I sent an application to the Australian Medical Council to take two exams to have my degree recognised. At the same time, I booked three English tests three months ahead to give me time to study for them. Two were IELTS (International English Language Testing System), the other was OET (Occupational English Test).

As I had software for IELTS I bought a printer and printed 4,000 pages for the English exam. I was reading them every day for three months whenever I got the chance. At the same time, I printed 1,000 pages for the medical exam and I was reading them too.

The Australian Medical Council sent back my application for the medical exam after six weeks, saying that my passport was missing my date of birth. I contacted the Iraqi embassy in Canberra. They said that at the end of January they would be in Broadmeadows, Melbourne where there was a large Iraqi community. I could get it changed there.

I turned up to take an English exam at Monash University after travelling from Albury the previous day. I was staying in a hotel near the Uni. To take the exam, I was required to show my passport, but I didn't have it. Despite travelling to Melbourne to get it changed, the Iraqi Embassy had taken my passport and still not returned it. All I had with me was a copy and hoped that this would suffice as the whole thing was costing around $500 – money I couldn't spare.

The Uni said, 'No, you're not allowed to sit the exam.' I was distraught and panicky, begging them to accept the copy. I explained that the embassy had delayed sending my passport back, but the answer was the same, 'No ID, no exam.'

Returning to the hotel, I felt exhausted and depressed. My future was uncertain. If I passed the exam, I would be able to apply for work. Now I felt hopeless. All that money and time wasted. Sitting in the hotel foyer, I took out my phone and recorded a video of my sad, sad face.

I said, 'Oh, Iraqi Embassy, now you do this to me!'

This recording would always be a reminder of a low time in my life. Whenever things got tough in the future I would play it back, but I was able to tell myself that however bad times things can get, there's a fresh new day tomorrow. You should live and feel the bitterness and disappointment when things go wrong but bounce back the next day because the hardship will not last.

It took four weeks for the embassy to make the necessary changes to my passport and I missed one of the English exams. I finally did the exams and passed the OET and the IELTS. I received a letter from the Medical Council who told me I was eligible to do the medical tests in April and July. I didn't apply for the exam because by then my visa would have expired and I would be back in Iraq.

Or so I thought...

Life in Albury and making friends

Life in Albury was good. In the first few weeks, the best thing that I noticed about Albury was that I could sleep at night. I was safe. I could just close my door and sleep soundly. The safety was a deeply satisfying feeling – a dream come true. I also started to eat better, and I could go out at night. And the electricity – I could have a hot shower every day, something extremely difficult in Iraq.

As my place was two hundred metres from Albury's main street, I would stroll down there. Almost immediately, I started to make friends. A restaurant called Canteen Cuisine was owned by a Lebanese man called Charlie, and Dimitri, a Greek, who were both in their early fifties. As I was going there frequently they started chatting to me, and we soon became friends. Charlie especially, being Arab, looked after me – feeding me good meals and cooking me whatever I wanted.

Dimitri, now one of my best friends, is very intelligent. He had studied medicine but dropped out after two years to join the army. He followed his wife to Australia in 1978 and never left. We had excellent conversations together and we would play chess on the sunny main street in the afternoons, especially around the Christmas holidays. Evenly matched, we became a bit of an institution; all the locals knew that we'd be out there. It's such a tradition now that whenever I go back to Albury, we have a game or two.

Dimitri took me to two pubs. One, the Zed Bar, is well known. Even though I was in my early thirties, I met Dimitri's older friends and enjoyed their company. Every time, Dimitri would ask me if I wanted a beer, but I always asked for a Coke. We'd laugh but he'd still ask. For me, alcohol wasn't permitted, and I felt uncomfortable when people became fighting drunk.

Dimitri and I, along with Tony, an Italian friend of Dimitri's, once went to another pub. There were many problems in Albury back then between the Aboriginal people and people with white skin. One drunken guy looked at me, asked me if I was Aboriginal, and was ready to punch me. Obviously my slightly darker skin was upsetting him. I told him I was Italian and never went back there.

Despite this incident I was safe and happy. I was starting to learn how to cook, so would call my mum and ask her what I should make and how. From time to time on a weekend, I'd visit Sam in Melbourne and do things like visit the zoo. Everyone was so different to Iraqis.

I found the Australians to be very kind. Australians accommodate people and are inclusive. They respected the fact that I didn't eat pork or drink alcohol, and that made it a good experience for me.

Applying for a refugee visa

In early February I went to Melbourne to do my English exam, and called my family to let them know I'd be returning home on 25 March. I was stunned and then distressed when my mother began to cry at my news. She told me not to come home because I'd certainly be kidnapped or killed.

With Sam out for dinner with one of his friends and the phone call on my mind, I wondered where I could go. Deciding to just spend time in the city, I walked from Flinders Street and followed some people who looked like they might be going to a sports event. Because my mind wasn't working properly, I arrived at the stadium and aimlessly bought a ticket. I've no idea who was playing, or what, for that matter – probably rugby. Everyone around me was drinking; I felt extremely restless, so I left.

Back at Sam's place, I just didn't know what to do. Sam advised me to go to an immigration agent and ask for help. The next day, on returning to Albury, I went on the internet and found an agent within walking distance from my unit. His name was Darren Reid.

Applying for a refugee visa

I found Darren to be an empathetic person. I explained my situation and my mother's warning, and he suggested that perhaps he could find me a job as a nurse. It was a nice idea, but I would never get a nursing job as I wasn't trained as one.

I asked him about a refugee visa, and he confessed that he'd never done an application for that. However, starting to leaf through a book on immigration law, he believed he could give it a shot if I gave him a week to read the law and then he'd let me know what I needed to do. Because he felt sorry for me, he waived the $5,000 minimum deposit for his services.

Leaving Darren, I went to the library, a favourite weekend haunt of mine, and found the book Darren had on immigration law. Copying all the relevant pages – fifty-five of them – I read and read until I became very familiar with them. Going back to Darren the following week, he was surprised to find that I knew more than he did. Putting our heads together, we went through the information and began collecting the required documents.

The process was arduous. Part of the application required me to state why I was a refugee. I'd spent three wonderful months in Australia trying to forget the violence of my past, and now I found myself trying to remember every single bad event that happened, every single friend that had been killed, along with my brother. I had to remember friends and family members who were persecuted, and the things that happened to me. I had to write down all those stories to convince the Immigration Department that I fell within the definition of a refugee.

It was heart-rending. I had tears streaming down my face as I wrote. Every sad and agonising memory that I'd managed to suppress welled up and became real again. It was an incredibly emotional time for me and, I suspect, the beginning of my need to write this book.

I contacted friends in Iraq and collected their letters and photos of our friends who'd been killed. Herbert, my supervisor, also wrote a moving letter, as did all the people I'd met in Australia along the way.

It was done.

Darren and I finished the application and submitted the visa request. Once I had submitted the application, I could stay on a bridging visa and could not be deported as, by law, the application for a full visa would be processed within ninety days.

Lecturing in neuroscience

In the meantime, I continued with my research. During that time, Herbert was teaching neuroscience to undergraduate physiotherapy, occupational therapy, and speech pathology students. He told me he was going overseas and had tried to get someone to present the lectures while he was away, but finding nobody available, he asked me if I thought I could do them.

I had only been four months in Australia by then, but I thought, 'Why not? I can do that.' He told me there would only be four lectures and three tutorials. I said I believed I could manage it.

He took me to the lecture theatre, and gave me a run down on the technology – the lights and the microphone and so on. He then introduced me to the students and informed them that the following week I would be giving the lectures and the tutorials.

The first tutorial – about the brain and how the nervous system works – was lightly attended with barely twenty students. The students just ignored me when I walked in. People were eating, laughing, talking loudly, and not looking at me at all. Standing at the front, I was astonished. In Iraq, the students stop talking immediately and stand when a lecturer enters the room.

I had to do something, so I wrote on the board, 'All the students who read this sentence should stand up.' Some stood immediately, others were hesitant and then stood, while others remained seated.

Waving them all back into their seats, I told the students that when I wrote that sentence on the board, their eyes detected the words and then converted the light into electrical impulses, which then moved to the back of the brain. That area processed the lights, sending another electrical impulse into the temporal lobe which was responsible for understanding reading. That area then sent another impulse to the frontal lobe, the decision-making area. I said that some of them understood what I'd written and decided they should obey, while others hesitated because they had different ideas.

And, I told them, some decided to stand up because the frontal lobe sent another impulse to the parietal lobe, the motor system responsible for movement. From that area, another electrical impulse went through the spinal cord to the muscles in the legs and the arms, signalling them to stand up.

I told them that when I waved my hand, their eyes understood what I was saying, and they sat down. I told them that all this happened in a very short time via the nervous system, which is a very complex part of the body. That was my way of introducing them to the brain, and that was what we'd be dealing with that semester. I had their attention.

It all happened in the moment. I didn't think about it, I just did it. I had to get the students to respect me and at the same time teach them a lesson without offence. It turned out to be a brilliant move. When I started the lectures, there were only twenty students out of 136. The second lecture was at capacity. By the end of the sessions, one of the lecturers told me I was Mr Popular because all the students attended my classes. But, in fact, it was because they understood what I was teaching them. When I explained, I would give examples and the students would leave with a good understanding of the subject. Neuroscience is a difficult concept, but I kept it very simple and I gave them plenty of clinical examples.

By the end of the four lectures, my supervisor returned and asked me if I would mind continuing the lectures until the end of the semester. After he told me that the students appeared to like my style, I agreed to do it. Herbert gave me his PowerPoint presentations and the book he used, and I had my own knowledge base in the area. Clinical examples and humour were the silver bullets, and Herbert would pay me for the lectures – a good thing, because once I finished the research I would no longer receive a salary.

Money worries

When I received the first $10,000 from the scholarship, I paid $7,200 in fees to the university, after I'd paid for travel and accommodation. Every month I received $2,500. Within two months, Hakeem asked me to send back his money because he needed it, so I sent him back $3,300. Despite Paryanta's help with budgeting, things were tough.

In March, my friend Berbouti called out of the blue. Berbouti was a GP in Canada. When he asked me how I was, I let him know that I was trying to do the exams to stay in Australia. 'Give me your bank account details,' he said. When I asked him why, he told me not to ask questions. He was going to send some money and urged me to do everything I could to stay in Australia and not return to Iraq. I hadn't even mentioned my financial situation, and

I still have no idea how he managed to get my phone number. 'Pay me back in the future,' he said. I was so relieved and grateful and used that money to support myself when my research finished.

Darren called to tell me that Immigration wanted to interview me in Sydney on 4 June 2008. My money was running out. I contacted one of my friends, Sinan, a radiologist from my university days in Iraq, and asked for help to get to the interview. He told me not to worry, then booked and paid for my flight, telling me I would stay with him in Sydney.

The immigration interview

At the interview to assess my request for refugee status, a Lebanese interpreter helped the interviewer who was Australian and second-generation Asian. I don't remember his name, but he was a very nice, though very tough, guy.

The interview brought up memories of hurtful and humiliating times. The interviewer asked difficult, searching questions and I almost broke down in tears.

I began to remember certain events, like having loaned a militiaman some money. When I asked him for it back, instead of thanking me, he dropped it on the floor in the hospital and, in front of many people, said, 'Here, I have put it under my shoe for you.' In Iraq, that is a deeply insulting thing to do and say. I couldn't show any feeling in front of the militiaman because to do so would probably result in my death. I had to swallow the shame and bitterness that I felt. Years later, the same man who had humiliated me contacted me from Turkey. He wanted me to sponsor him to come to Australia. I could have told the government that he was a dangerous character, but I didn't. I simply stopped all contact with him and let God make the decision.

More memories came flooding back, and I felt overwhelmed by sadness. The immigration officer would listen to me, and then calmly put a tick in a box. The interpreter's eyes were full of tears, she couldn't help herself. 'Oh, that life was very tough. I wish ...' she said, and had to stop because she was supposed to have neutral feelings. Speaking in English, I used the interpreter only once when I couldn't think of a particular word.

I had to remember and narrate all the terrible things that had happened to me in my life in Iraq. I had to convince the immigration officer that it was a perilous place to live, so I couldn't hold back.

The immigration officer asked me how it was that I was a doctor and my brother a PhD but we weren't part of Saddam's regime. He said only Saddam's people went to university: I told him I was ranked eighth in Iraq with my final school exams. When he asked why I didn't go to medical school, I told him that all people who got high marks went to university, not just Saddam's people. After finishing the interview, I left, and the interpreter followed. She was wiping away tears and told me she felt sad for me and wished me all the best.

I returned to Albury, and on 12 June, Darren phoned and asked me to come to his office. When I arrived, he told me that the immigration officer who'd interviewed me wanted to talk to me on the phone. Taking the phone, I was very nervous – but incredibly relieved and delighted when he told me that in the name of the Immigration Minister I was being granted a permanent protection visa. Congratulating me, he wished me all the best in Australia, and from the way he said it, it was from the heart.

I phoned Saleem to tell him and my family that I was staying. They were hugely relieved.

This picture was taken in June 2008 after the interview with immigration for refugee status.

A new job

By then, having paid eight weeks' rent, I had only $125 left. I phoned Sinan, asking him if he could lend me $1,000. When that ran out, Sam helped me with $1,000. All this was calculated on the basis that Herbert would pay me for the lectures and tutorials.

I finished the last lecture and was relieved that I'd managed financially during that time. But, as the AMC (Australian Medical Council) exam was coming up in July, I asked Berbouti for help with the $1,800 I needed to sit for it. He sent it to me.

Waiting for Herbert one day, another lecturer, Harriet, asked me if I was interested in doing more university teaching. When I said that I was keen, she asked about my knowledge of anatomy and physiology. I told her that I was very good at them, so she went off to speak to Julia Coyle, Head of the School.

Ten minutes later, I was in Julia's office, where she told me that the university was twenty years old and in all that time the student feedback for physiotherapy lecturers had never been good. For the first time in the history of the school the feedback on the lecturer *had* been good – and that lecturer was me.

Julia offered me a full-time job as a lecturer for five months. 'What do you think?' she asked. Well, I had no money and I was borrowing from my friends, so I said, 'Of course I'll accept.' That was incredibly good news and Julia arranged a contract for me to sign. I had been almost penniless and suddenly I had a full-time job. Herbert then paid me for the lectures I'd done, which helped me pay the rent and cover living costs.

I went off to Melbourne to sit the first part of the AMC exam and passed it. Back in Albury, I started my lecturing and was paid for both teaching and preparation time. Teaching microbiology, anatomy, physiology, exercise physiology, and human science students, I was reading one day and lecturing the next which allowed me to do a good job.

My first day teaching anatomy was the first time I'd been in an anatomy lab since medical school in 1995. In anatomy, you use a cadaver (a human body) to explain every structure to the students. It's often difficult to see when there are so many students crowding around. To get around that, I had read every anatomy book and studied the pictures. In a flash all that knowledge came back to me exactly how I'd read it and I was able to explain every structure over and over until the students got it.

One day, a strange thing happened. Explaining something to my students, I turned and saw myself in a mirror. There I was in a gown, teaching. I couldn't believe it. For a split second I faltered. 'Oh, my God,' I thought. 'How did I manage to get all the way here and be teaching medical students in Australia?' It was both the weirdest and scariest feeling at the same time. I quickly turned my face, but it was a long time before I could look in that mirror again.

A new job

*

My teaching was fifteen hours a week, so I wasn't busy. The rest of the time I'd mark assignments, do my own studies, or prepare lectures. Between lectures I was quite free, and that was liberating. My regular income allowed me to save hard and pay back my debts to my friends in Sydney and Melbourne. My Canadian benefactor was paid back in full the following year when my income stream strengthened. I owe a huge debt of gratitude to those people – bailing me out in such tight times saved my life, literally.

In my second week of full-time work, Tim, my friend in the UK, moved to Australia. When he visited me, we spent two solid days without sleep, just talking and talking because we hadn't seen each other for six years. We shared our stories of what had happened to us both during that time. He told me about the British lady he'd met and a few weeks later she followed him to Australia. I was proud to be a witness to their marriage.

Three months later, they returned to the UK because his wife was missing her family. It was disappointing for us both. Tim also wanted to become a specialist in Australia because the training is more thorough and international students can join the programs. When they went back, as Tim was now married to a British citizen, he was allowed British citizenship and could then begin training. He's presently an emergency consultant.

*

I enjoyed the teaching, and the students enjoyed my lectures and tutorials, but I was eager to don my stethoscope again and get back to the clinical environment of being a doctor. With the first part of the AMC exam out of the way, I was eligible to apply for jobs as a doctor. I decided to focus on public hospitals in Victoria and New South Wales as I was more familiar with those states. Using my copy of the directory of public hospitals as a guide, I sent my CV everywhere.

I did apply to some hospitals in Queensland, but they required the second part of the exam be completed. The AMC was different back then. With so many people applying for the exam, there was a rule that you had to wait two years for a shot at the second part, so it would be two years before Queensland would look at my applications.

My phone interview for a Mildura hospital, a prosperous town around eight hours from Albury, was a failure. I had no idea how to handle an interview – it just didn't work that way in Iraq. Graduation over there guaranteed a job and career, and advancement from then on. It's a completely exam-results-driven system and very competitive. The higher a student's average, the more likely they'd get their choice of position.

Applying to the Albury hospital, again I didn't succeed at the interview. Everyone was asking for Australian experience, which was obviously a bit of a problem. My third attempt was as a GP in an Albury clinic, but I couldn't see myself in that role and backed away.

My lectures and tutorials contract ended in November and I was unemployed. My applications continued but around then I began receiving auto-replies to say that they'd be considered after the New Year.

With decent savings and a low rent, I wasn't too concerned. I was determined to be a doctor, so I left it to God. I'd survived Iraq, so surviving Australia wasn't an issue. Anyway, another important part of my life was about to unfold.

Jenny

Albury is pleasant around Christmas – summer and sunshine. I had friends and spent a great deal of time enjoying the days with Dimitri and Charlie. I also contacted my family on a weekly basis, although in those days there was only the expensive mobile. It's so much better now with free calls and video connections.

On 2 December, I met Jenny, a Korean student at the university. During the Christmas holidays, most of the international students travelled back to their homes, as do many students from Melbourne and other places in Australia. But Jenny had stayed. She wanted to work and save money, and was doing two jobs: one in a Chinese restaurant for fifteen hours a week, and the other in a sushi takeaway in the mornings until midday. It seemed like Jenny and I were the only university people left in Albury.

I was in the main street in front of my favourite restaurant when I saw Jenny and recognised her as one of the students. I recalled that one day when I was teaching the anatomy class about the position of all the muscles in a cadaver, Jenny was standing away from the other students with a friend, studying pictures in

Jenny

an anatomy book. It immediately reminded me of when I was a medical student in 1995. A couple of friends and I couldn't get close enough to the cadaver because of other students pushing themselves too tightly around it. Because we only had the pictures to follow, it was difficult to remember the lessons, and my marks suffered in the practical exams. Understanding immediately what was happening with Jenny and her friend, I called them over and explained that she wouldn't learn properly from a book alone and stood them at the front.

When I saw her, it was 4.55 pm and she was due to start her Chinese restaurant job at five. But I learnt quite a bit about her in those few minutes.

I discovered that she was twenty-nine and single. I was thirty-two, so it seemed like a good fit. With her being from overseas and stuck in Albury over Christmas, we had quite a bit in common.

Jenny had been a practising physiotherapist in Korea but couldn't practise here until she studied in an Australian university – very much like my situation.

As she was telling me a little about studying in Australia, I noticed that she had lovely eyes, jet-black hair and fair skin. In fact, she was extremely attractive. When I asked her if we could be friends, she said, 'Why not?'

On that first day, Jenny went to her work and, luckily for me, mentioned our brief meeting to a friend there who encouraged her to explore our relationship. I had a good reputation at the university and the fact that I'd arrived from Iraq and started lecturing almost immediately impressed Jenny, who also dreamed of attaining a professorship and lecturing. On our second day, we went to Charlie and Dimitri's restaurant together.

It was fun, and a bit like being on holiday. Taking advantage of the good weather, we went out and about and got to know each other. I had an emergency course with advanced life support already booked in at Shepparton Hospital in December, so I was away for a few days, but we chatted over the phone and developed a stronger bond. Jenny's friend had travelled back to Korea around that time, leaving her car with Jenny, so we began to explore the towns around Albury. At a wildlife place called Ettamogah, I saw a kangaroo for the first time. It was a perfect time to get to know one another.

We spent Christmas Day together. There wasn't a soul on the streets, reminding me of Baghdad when curfews stopped everyone going out on Fridays. Muslim prayers on Friday afternoons, called Friday Prayers, are a bit like Sunday church services for Christians. The government introduced curfews because they had been unable to solve the problem of car bombs and the high danger posed to citizens. Initially they said that no cars could be on the streets, but walking would be OK. But after bombs went off at three different mosques with hundreds of people dying, the government decided that they couldn't protect the people, especially as the police were ineffective. The curfews made the streets very quiet.

One of the things we didn't have in common was our religion, but I never take a person's religion into consideration when it comes to friendship. Although I'm very religious, religion isn't a factor that influences whether a person is good or bad. Many people pretend to be religious but they can be malicious and violent. Religion didn't matter for me, but cultural differences did. There are times Jenny and I don't understand each other because of our cultural differences, which makes our relationship interesting. Jenny is a non-practising Christian but believes in God, something important to me.

Jenny and me.

One day, Dimitri took Jenny and me to a club where he was a member; the SS&A (Sailors, Soldiers and Airmen's) Club. It was full; it seemed that all of Albury was there. Waiting for our meal, Jenny asked me what things made me happy. When I told her that I didn't want to be happy and felt that I'd never find happiness, she was understandably shocked. There was complete silence.

Despite all the wonderful things happening to me, I was actually severely depressed and couldn't stop thinking about my family. I admitted that after everything that had happened, I couldn't see how happiness would ever factor into my life. The concept was beyond my comprehension.

I recently asked Jenny about that time compared to now. She told me that sometimes we'd go out for lunch and although the food and environment were excellent, I'd just be thinking about my family and the mood would plummet into blackness. That's when Jenny couldn't imagine what would ever make me happy. Finally, she figured out that I wasn't really interested in material possessions like cars or a house, but it was simple things that made me happy. She said that if we were out walking around sunset, or we felt breezes similar to the ones I remembered from Baghdad, I would feel happiness. It sounds very much like our early days together were horrible for her.

Not a party girl, Jenny had come to Australia to find a new life. She was supported by her parents who paid the high university fees but felt like a burden for them, and took on two jobs to help. Jenny is a very organised and meticulous person. She is very kind and caring. When we met, both of us felt that we had known each other for a long time. We enjoyed our time together and I no longer felt lonely.

Lecturing

In January, I was still applying for jobs. I had a call from my university supervisor, asking me if I was interested in lecturing in two subjects and being paid around a $1,000 for nine hours per week. That was brilliant, but did raise a problem with my developing relationship with Jenny. She was a student and I was on staff. Because Jenny wasn't attending any of my lectures and there was no conflict of interest, we decided I'd accept and we'd keep our relationship discreet.

By the end of February, I'd still had no luck getting a hospital job. Finally, a job opportunity appeared for a full-time lecturer at the university for four years, and I was granted an interview for it. One of the five interviewers, a lady running one of the subjects, asked me where I saw myself in five years. I answered honestly, but very badly. In Iraq, five years into the future is unimaginable.

Because life is so tenuous, we can think only one day ahead. If tomorrow is all right, we can think about the next day. Still in that mindset, all I wanted was a job in order to have sufficient money to live and continue my quest to become a doctor. The university was looking for someone on course for a PhD, or who would benefit the institution one day.

I failed the interview, and it was a good thing for me. Committing to lecturing for three to five years at a university would not have been to my advantage. I am much happier being a doctor, a clinician.

I don't think I gave any answer in the interview that would have scored well. Maybe one or two, but because of how I thought, I would never have comprehended what they wanted and given an appropriate answer. Later, after years of experience and many interviews, I began to understand what was going on. I had no plans and I needed to be prepared. It was Jenny who put me right. When I came back from the interview, and told her about the questions and my answers, she told me I wouldn't be getting the job.

She explained about having plans, and that started me thinking. I realised that I needed to understand my weaknesses and try harder to adjust to my new country.

Job offer and separation

Luckily, within a few days I received an email from Warragul Hospital. I'd sent my CV to them a few months previously but they said they didn't have any positions. Now, a doctor had resigned and they wanted to interview me for the position.

Seven hours of travel later, I was presented with a scenario involving an ECG (electrocardiogram), an instrument deployed when a patient has a heart attack. That was my specialty so it was easy for me. Confidently giving my answers with all the possibilities and treatments, I knew that few interviewees would have such in-depth knowledge. But it wasn't going to be that easy.

When they asked me about my Australian medical experience, I was irritated and lost my temper. I asked them how I could get Australian experience when hospitals wouldn't give me a job because I didn't have Australian experience. Strangely, and although they were surprised at my passionate response, that was a good answer as far they were concerned. I added that I'd been teaching complex medical subjects at the university for a year and had no trouble with English, so I finished my interview, collected my bags and set off for the long trip home.

Midway back, the train broke down and buses were brought for us. While waiting for the bus, I received a phone call from Simon Fraser, Director of Medical Services in Warragul, telling me he'd like to offer me a job as a medical officer starting on 23 April 2009. After waiting for seven months to get a job offer, I couldn't believe it. I was shocked into silence.

Simon finally asked me what I thought and would I accept the offer. My senses returned and I told him, 'Yes, of course!' Simon asked me to send him all the required paperwork and he'd email me to confirm the offer. I then settled back to thoroughly enjoy the journey home and, I must admit, I smiled … quite a bit.

After working my four weeks' notice at the university, I left for Warragul with the faculty's understanding. They knew I was following my life's ambition to become a doctor and wished me well. On the other hand, Jenny thought our relationship was at an end.

Distances aren't anything to me. With friends and family in many countries, I always keep in close touch. Jenny was important to my life and it never occurred to me for a moment that we'd fall apart because of a separation. When I told her this, and that I'd be back in Albury whenever I could, she was pessimistic and said, 'Let's see.'

Whenever I had two days free I went back to Albury. With Jenny, Dimitri, Charlie and many acquaintances there, it was my home. Warragul was completely different. There it was work and I had no friends outside the hospital.

When Jenny and I had gone out for the first time, I was unemployed. My single unit had a mattress on the floor and wasn't exactly luxurious. Jenny did not for a moment judge me. She respected what she saw in me, my knowledge and achievements; the fact that I had no money or that my religion was different wasn't important to her.

Getting to know Jenny, I soon saw not just her beauty but recognised her strengths. She worked and studied so hard – far harder than me. Ploughing on with two jobs and determined to finish university, Jenny won my respect.

I had met Iraqi girls in Australia before meeting Jenny. One of them had lived in Australia from childhood. We were sitting in a café one day when she lit a cigarette. Having just arrived from Iraq and speaking my mind directly, I asked her why she was smoking. I don't think she appreciated that too much, but she told me that she smoked because in Australia men and women are equal. I was shocked. Not by the equality thing – that I agree with. It was that she'd taken all the wonderful concepts of equality and could only demonstrate her support of them by doing something unhealthy and unpleasant. Equality is the right to study, the right to job and pay equality, and shared home duties. It's about positive things.

I'm lucky because I had more time to get to know Jenny and for her to know me. Like everyone, I had my faults but she liked me regardless. And it wasn't all plain sailing. Because of our cultural differences, we had a lot of fights and disagreements until we got to know more of each other. However, at the end of the day we became more comfortable by bringing our differences into the open.

Whenever I heard an ambulance siren, I'd have a panic attack. Jenny would anticipate that and hold my hand or hug me. She knows me more than anyone. Our relationship will be lasting because we can build on what we have.

When people see me at Jenny's clinic they ask her if I'm Muslim. When she tells them I'm an Iraqi Muslim, they ask her how much I hit her and how badly I treat her. Jenny laughs because she knows that I've never shouted at anyone in my life and will always back away from any physical confrontation. I'm not here to fight: I'm here to help and heal.

Warragul Hospital

After I left for Warragul, Jenny told me that she thought she'd never see me again. In fact, just four weeks later, I made the first of many trips back there. It became a routine – when I had two or three days off, I was off to see Jenny. And, when she had time off, she'd often be over to stay with me.

Our relationship continued and, admittedly, it was hard – yet good in some ways. With much to discuss between visits, our relationship developed deeper meaning. Jenny could also study on weekdays and I'd interrupt her only on weekends. And, around

Warragul, there were beautiful lake and bush walks where we could spend our time.

Warragul Hospital is a small seventy-seven bed hospital with medical, surgical, paediatric and obstetrics services. I was working in the emergency department; I was happy there. In the emergency area, there were eight doctors who had graduated overseas and a few interns (new doctors) from Frankston and Monash universities, with one GP who supervised us.

In Iraq, we would see the patient within one or two minutes; they were examined and their history would be taken down very quickly. In the time we saw one patient in Australia, we would have seen four in Iraq. Here, I was spending thirty to forty minutes to see one patient with everything documented and a plan in place.

With solid experience behind me and around sixty percent of the emergency cases being medical, I was in my element. Another twenty percent were surgical and ten percent paediatric with very few obstetric, gynaecological or women's health cases. Iraq had taught me to see patients and diagnose quickly. Now I had the bonus of getting x-rays done before 11 pm and blood tests before 5 pm.

The emergency department nursing staff were very efficient and knew their stuff, sometimes more than the doctors. Coming from the local community, they had energy and spirit. I soon realised that they also liked working with me because I was clear and built their confidence up. When I found out that some nurses were specifically trying to work with me, I felt flattered and humbled.

As a doctor, I understood the way the emergency department worked – something patients are unaware of. Sometimes doctors are reluctant to make a decision so keep a patient overnight for a specialist to see them the next morning.

One night, I had a sick female doctor come in. I knew I had to ignore her medical background and her attempts to lead the diagnosis. After spending twenty minutes asking her many questions about her symptoms, I told her it was a kidney stone. It being late, I couldn't get blood work or x-rays done so I wrote up her notes, gave her medication for the pain, and rather than keep her in overnight as the other doctors would, I sent her home and asked her to come back in the morning.

The next morning, my supervisor saw her, a scan was done, and they could see the kidney stone. My supervisor told me that he was impressed by my assessment. The patient had come in the previous night afraid that her condition was appendicitis or that something was wrong with her ovaries, but she was totally reassured by my assessment because I'd asked all the right questions and given her some pain relief and a clear plan.

One day a patient came to emergency with diarrhoea. Asking numerous questions as I examined him, I concluded that he had a bowel obstruction, something that necessitates immediate admission for surgery. Because of the diarrhoea, the attending nurse was unconvinced and asked what it was I intended to do. I told her the patient needed an x-ray. She reluctantly called the radiologist who found the suspected blockage.

I believe I proved myself to be a good doctor and diagnostician. I was always calm and quiet because in Iraq I was surrounded by war and chaos. This had taught me to be focused, even in the middle of madness. While many of Warragul's emergency doctors were stressed, the relatively peaceful environment was heaven to me. Equipment, medication, and staff at my fingertips – wonderful!

Overnight, I might be the only doctor in the hospital for emergency and admission, and for the inpatients who needed help during the night. I had seven nightshifts every couple of months; I struggled for the first few because I had to learn the computer system. In Iraq, we didn't have consultants available during the night and just had to manage by ourselves. In the Australian system, there's a certain way doctors must talk to consultants about patients and I had to learn that.

One night, a nurse from the ward called me about a patient in her early sixties who had become unwell. She was sitting at the edge of her bed, holding on to it and hardly able to breathe. She was exhausted. I immediately diagnosed her with emphysema and unless we put her on a tube and ventilator, she would die.

The nurse told me that the patient had been like that for fifteen minutes, and asked if she could give her morphine. That would have killed her. When I explained that the patient needed a tube inserted, not morphine, the nurse was surprised. Unused to overseas doctors with emergency skills, she assumed I wouldn't know what to do.

The nurse said that if the patient needed a tube, I would have to call the consultant, Dr Wright, a man with a reputation for being grumpy when called at night. When I called him at 4 am with the patient's symptoms and said that she needed a tube, he laughed at me because in Australia, diagnosis isn't done without all the necessary tests being done. It's protocol.

The consultant suggested that maybe she was having a heart attack, so an ECG was required – or maybe her decreased level of consciousness indicated a low blood sugar, so a blood sugar test was needed. I also had to test for levels of carbon dioxide, which I asked the nurse to do. The blood gas came back with the carbon dioxide at 129 where normal was around 40.

Having the evidence to support my diagnosis within five minutes, I told the nurse not to worry about the other tests and was back onto Dr Wright. 'Shit,' he said. 'You're right, she needs a tube. I'm on my way.'

Our patient was saved and on a plane to a city hospital. Untreated, and with obstructed breathing forcing her to use her muscles to keep the air flowing, she would have probably gone into cardiac arrest and died. It was a good lesson for me to always do the tests to support what I was thinking, and before I called a consultant.

At the end of each year working in emergency, all the emergency doctors had to do five weeks on the wards. There, we looked after patients admitted by their GPs when the GPs weren't there, checking their medication and doing the required paperwork.

This came with an unexpected outcome.

The medical team from Monash

On the ward, there was also a medical team in training from Monash University looking after their own patients. The teams of two registrars, two interns and three physicians arrived every ten weeks or so.

Every week Ken, the pharmacist, gave a presentation to the doctors, including the Monash team. One week, he did a quiz about drugs used for diabetes. When no one could answer the second question, I answered it and then answered most of the following questions. It surprised the registrars, who were theoretically the most knowledgeable.

A couple of days later, the registrars were doing a physician's exam on the computer while I was working nearby. Hearing them discussing a question they couldn't answer, I told them that the particular case was familial hypocalciuric hypercalcemia, and that it ran in families. I went on to tell them why I'd come to that conclusion, and what tests to run to diagnose it. On checking the answer, they found I was correct and asked me to do many more, which I answered correctly.

Curious, they asked me about my background and, after I'd told them about Iraq and my studies, they left.

But I had not heard the last of it.

True ambassador

The medical team leader went to see Dr Bruce Maydom about me. Dr Maydom had a reputation for being very stern. When he walked into a ward, everyone quickly disappeared. In the mornings, the doctors doing their handover had to be very careful what they said and how they said it because he could be easily upset. At the same time, he was very good with his patients and looked after them very well.

Dr Maydom went to the nursing staff in emergency to talk to them about me, and then came to see me. Telling me he'd heard a lot about me, he asked about my previous experience, training, and studies before asking if I'd like to join the medical team and be a registrar – a huge promotion that normally took a few more years.

Joining the medical team meant a lot more responsibility, more than becoming boss of the emergency team. Within a few weeks, I signed a new contract for $40 an hour as opposed to the $30 I'd been receiving. The emergency department were upset that I was leaving but they couldn't argue with Dr Maydom because he was tough and powerful within the hospital.

*

For the six months that I was with the medical team as a registrar, there were three consultants: Dr Bruce Maydom, Dr Mort Fitzgerald and Dr Brett Forge. Older and extremely knowledgeable, they're all still working there, many years later.

Dr Mort Fitzgerald is the nicest person I have ever met in my life. His manners are impeccable, and he can't annoy anyone. Dr Forge has vast cardiology knowledge and loves to play tennis. Called in at eleven at night, he'll still be wearing his tennis shorts, having abandoned a game. To begin with, I was quite scared of Dr Bruce Maydom. But I quickly discovered how he likes things done and how kind he is with patients and how he knows every single detail about them. I soon started to get on well with him.

I was privileged to work with these three consultants for six months. The other registrars from Monash would stay for thirteen weeks and then would go. The consultants soon realised that I managed the patients well, was reliable, and only called them when they were really needed. Doing a case presentation in one of our Thursday meetings, I was both happy and very embarrassed when Dr Forge said, 'Issam has raised the standard of the meetings.'

Eight years later, one of my presentations – on how to manage diabetic ketoacidosis, a life-threatening condition – is still remembered. Four percent of people die from this condition in Iraq because there are no blood tests for it. In Australia, the protocol is to put the person in ICU or in the high dependency area and do blood tests every hour. I couldn't do that in Iraq. There was just me to manage over one hundred cases. My only way to save patients was by my clinical examinations and measuring everything I could – their physiological changes, their body weight.

The doctors told me to stop the presentation because I was teaching bad medicine. No wonder it's remembered!

My work in Warragul was about proving myself day by day, working hard and staying calm. A registrar's job comes with one intern, and the consultant comes when there's a clinic. I was looking after between ten and twenty patients during the day. Every day I would see them to adjust their management plan and perhaps change their medications, until they got better and could go home.

One day, not long before Christmas in 2010, a lady around seventy was admitted with pneumonia. I went to see her, and she asked me where I was from. Before I left, she asked me if she would be well enough before Christmas to go on a holiday to Paris. I gently patted her on her leg and told her not to worry, that she would be in Paris before Christmas.

My reassuring manner with smiles, laughter and kindness helped her a lot. And I do that with every patient. I talk nicely and kindly and I keep a human touch with them. Sometime later, that lady sent a card to the hospital to say how I'd affected her and how lovely the nurses and medical team were. And that she got to Paris for Christmas!

The card that she sent read:

To the tall and handsome Iraqi Doctor, in his beautiful blue shirts, who treated me with compassion and humour. Life, I would think, had not always been easy for him and yet he showed such kindness. I wish him well, whether it is here in Australia, or back in his home country, of which he is a true Ambassador.

Dr Bruce Maydom came in ten minutes after the card arrived, and seeing it, asked me what I'd done. Surprised, I told him I'd done nothing unusual. He said that he'd worked at Warragul Hospital for thirty years and he had never received a card like that, and that I should keep it. He asked more about me and I told him some stories about Iraq. He was very interested and asked me to work with him on weekends, so he could hear more. He then asked me to present some of my stories to the Friday meetings which all the staff and local GPs attended.

At the end of 2010, I did the AMC clinical exam and passed. Deciding that it was time to move on from Warragul, I tendered three-month's notice. With my AMC registration, I could work anywhere.

Before I left, with Jenny supporting me, and introduced by Dr Maydom, I gave a PowerPoint presentation entitled 'Doctor from Baghdad', about how I saved the hospital in Iraq, and how it came about that hospitals in Iraq were made public with free hospital care. I included evidence like scanned newspaper articles about me, and told everyone about friends who were killed and kidnapped, and how I ended up in Warragul.

In the presentation, I put the card addressed 'to the tall, handsome Iraqi doctor' on the first page. When it came up, Dr Maydom joked that he'd thought I was a humble person and why was I putting up the card. Laughing, I told them that it was because of the card that Dr Maydom had forced me to do the presentation.

At the end of the presentation, every single person stood up and clapped for ten minutes without pause. I told them that when I arrived at Warragul all I wanted was a simple job working in emergency; they were touched, and everyone came by to shake my hand. The consultants were impressed, telling me that I should consider training to become a physician and then come back as a consultant – I'd always have a permanent job waiting for me there.

One month later I left, and travelled back to Iraq for a few weeks.

Leaving Warragul, and beyond

The nursing staff in emergency decided to give me a farewell party at a staff member's house. At the party, I was presented with an Australian flag and a photo of me eating biscuits on Australia Day labelled 'Honorary Australian'. They were proud of me, and I think my work, knowledge and kindness had been appreciated. I was humbled when they chanted 'Aussie, Aussie, Aussie, Oy, Oy, Oy!' as if celebrating my being Australian even before I'd become an Australian citizen.

Also, Dr Bruce Maydom invited me to dinner at a restaurant with Dr Forge and Dr Fitzgerald. That's how I left Warragul – feeling supported and with more experience and confidence.

During the months before I left Warragul, I'd had an offer of GP work in Albury and an interview with Western Health in Melbourne. It was a medical registrar's job, which is also part of the physician's training. In the interview, Elke, the director of training, met me and asked me what I expected the difference between a rural area and the city would be. By now, I was more confident, telling her that I expected to see more complex cases and that more resources would be available compared with rural areas. I also expected more training. They called to offer me a job and I was delighted.

Now I could start physician training – but first I needed Jenny's support. It would mean almost starting from scratch again; the training would involve another six years of exams and long working hours. It wouldn't be easy, but Jenny knew how important it was for me, and was behind me all the way.

If all went well, I'd finish my training in August 2017 and get the letters of certification at the end of that year. In America, only four years of extra training are needed to become a specialist. In Australia, we're required to work a year or two before joining the six-year training program. However, there's no way the training can be completed in six years – more like seven. So, I was looking at another ten years before becoming a specialist.

Training in Australia versus in Iraq

Australian training would make me better experienced than my colleagues in Iraq. In fact, there's no comparison. Sometimes, one of my Iraqi doctor friends will call me for an opinion when one of their relatives gets sick. Because I look at every single angle to get the big picture, they know that I manage my patients well.

One day, my friend from the UK contacted me to tell me his father in Baghdad had suffered a heart attack and intended to travel to India for by-pass surgery. Six hours before the flight, his father experienced some symptoms. I was sent the blood test results at two in the morning. I immediately realised that he was bleeding in the bowel as a result of his medication. If he travelled he would run into serious trouble.

I contacted his son, and told him to cancel the flight and get his father into hospital. I told him about the bleeding in the bowel and to stop the medication. I was correct. The hospital found the bleeding and his life was saved. I guided the treatment for six weeks until the father was able to travel and told him how to contact the consultant in India to tell him about the situation.

The father travelled without any problems and had the surgery. He then developed complications, and I guided the treatment there too. Getting him stabilised, I eventually got him well enough to go back to Baghdad where he developed fluid on the lungs.

The surgeons wanted to operate to remove the fluid and I refused, giving them an alternative treatment. After a few weeks, the fluid went and I could introduce the appropriate medications for heart recovery. He's now at a good exercise level, walking regularly, going to the mosque, and symptom free.

Although the patient had seen many doctors in Iraq, he never received the right advice. The doctors there don't see the big picture and they don't plan. From the first day, I planned to have him back to exercising. Not just to remove the shortness of breath: I wanted to improve his heart and within six months for him to be able to do things that he couldn't do before.

Another friend's father in Dubai had bowel cancer. Initially, my friend asked me about chemotherapy. Because his father was at an advanced age, I suggested that he stop the chemotherapy and do conservative management. Later, he was admitted to hospital with heart problems, angina and chest pain. He also had a damaged kidney.

The doctors didn't consider the patient's best interests. They wanted to do an angiogram using contrast media or dye, which could destroy his kidneys. Then the patient would require dialysis. That does not fix the heart problem. He was getting chest pain because he was losing blood from the bowel; if the bowel was stented, blood thinners would be required and that would create more bleeding. It was all a delicate roundabout and much needed to be considered.

I instructed them to use a specific medication to improve the blood, and certain other medications to control the symptoms. My friend's father went from having chest pains every five minutes to being able to go home after a couple of weeks. He was still going to succumb to the cancer, but that would be a good couple of years later.

The training that I got in Australia was good and thorough. It is truly holistic. My friend's father in Baghdad was a very religious person and his main purpose in life was to go to the mosque and pray. That was all he wanted to live for and it made him happy. My plan was to get him to a level of health to achieve that. His son was unable to see that as a treatment goal.

In Australia, we try to achieve goals to make the patient happy. It's not just the goal of no pain or to prolong life: it's about the quality of life and having some meaning in it. My Iraqi colleagues are beginning to appreciate that now – but I now have a problem because everyone wants to call me to discuss their issues.

The medical training here is focused on values, goals and patient rights, as well as consideration for their families. This is a different way of thinking and a different way of doing things, and everything about it seems to work for me and suits my way of thinking and passion. The health system here provides a doctor with everything to enable the best job that will have the best possible outcome for all.

It turns out I'm happy – really happy.

Returning to Iraq

In November of 2009 I had saved enough to repay all my debts with some left over, and had annual leave owing. Badly missing my family, it was time to take a trip back to Iraq. I booked a flight to Jordan to see my brother first, intending to go on to Baghdad after that. The prospect scared me but I was determined to do it.

I planned to spend the night at my brother Saleem's home when I arrived in Jordan, but I wasn't allowed to enter the country. Although I had refugee travel documents – a United Nations passport with an Australian visa – and I was from Australia, which the Jordanian authorities respected, they wouldn't budge.

However, they allowed me to stay at a hotel at the airport where I could meet my brother and his family. Seeing him, I started to cry but he hugged me and told me I was a man and to stop crying. That wasn't entirely possible. After all that time, my feelings were flooding crazily. My eyes still fill with tears when I remember it now. I hadn't seen my brother for four years, so we made the most of the hour we spent together.

The next day, I flew on to Baghdad. Arriving there I felt a mishmash of feelings that are now hard to comprehend, but the strongest was sadness when I entered my home. It had been almost destroyed, needed a lot of renovation, and my family weren't able to do any repairs because nobody was working. There was my mother in her room, surrounded by the remnants of her home. The scene was incredibly forlorn.

I gave my mother $9,000, and it was used wisely. She gave the cash to Mohammad, my younger brother, who had a business buying children's clothes from China and selling them in Baghdad's main market. He was a very good business man – even people with shops bought from him. Later, as the business expanded, he travelled regularly to China and circumstances greatly improved at home.

On my second visit in 2010, I took more money. Two days before I arrived, my mother had gone to Mecca so my brother Hakeem and I decided to renovate the entire house. We spent two weeks renovating from eight in the morning to very late at night. Renovating the bathroom meant no showering for a few days – I missed the Australian luxury that I was already taking for granted.

The day before my mother came back, we worked until one in the morning just cleaning up. Getting the rugs back in place very early the next day was the icing on the cake. When my mother walked in, she said, 'Oh, you guys, what did you do?' She was over the moon. The interior is no longer dark, which has completely changed the atmosphere. The colours have lightened everyone's mood enormously. Making those small changes to their lives was immensely satisfying.

About a year later, my brother Hakeem became depressed; the doctors didn't care and treated him poorly, exposing him to a lot of unnecessary tests and treatment. Taking over his management was difficult. I'd receive calls from him at two, three or four in the morning with constant panic attacks. I worked with him for three years, and he's now in a good place in life. The panic attacks are infrequent and he's able to move on. I support him financially too, which takes considerable stress away.

My trips to Iraq aren't jaunts; they're to give my family a better life. Before the war, we were a poor family but always lived a decent life. We had a big house and we had dignity. My mother has endured so much sadness but at least she is comfortable in her house now. The soul is back. The house is bright and it raises the family spirits. When relatives come to visit, my family are happy to bring them inside.

My visits to Iraq are not without considerable risk. I can go back for a week or two but I don't think I would survive for two months. It would be a miracle. Recently a twelve-year-old girl went back to Iraq on a visit and was killed. She was just part of the population and nobody special to target.

On a recent visit, I came out of the airport to find there were no taxis. Government buses arrived to take us two kilometres away to get public transport. Half-way there, a massive explosion occurred nearby and I really wondered if I was doing the right thing by going back.

If I went to the university, I had to hide myself and avoid anyone who had links to the militia because they might kidnap me. It was a real possibility. A couple of years earlier, a man from Malaysia went back to the hospital and was kidnapped. Malaysia is not perceived as a wealthy place but the kidnappers still demanded $250,000. Being Australian, I'm a tempting target and Jenny worries that whenever I go, I won't make it back.

I've now been in Australia long enough to stand out in Iraq, and that's dangerous. It's the simple things that could be my downfall: one day, I instinctively thanked the bus driver. People were surprised and stared because nobody says 'thank you' there, especially not to bus drivers.

Sometimes, my brothers will not allow me to talk in public because I'll be noticed.

Not all my friends return to Baghdad. Only one other friend and I have the nerve and motivation. My family's spirits are lifted when I go back and that's as important for me as it is medicine for them.

However, it's becoming increasingly difficult to go, and with my mother's age and health, a harder decision. There's no health system there, so people my mother's age can easily succumb to the slightest infection. They won't go to a hospital either because that's often a one-way street. Those things are complicated by Jenny and I having two young children now.

These are difficult choices.

Melbourne Western Health Hospital

In 2011, my physician training started. The six-year program comprises three years of basic training and three years of advanced. I had to pass a theory and a practical or clinical exam in the third year before I could go on to the advanced training.

The training starts from February, with two semesters divided into four terms for rotation. Every three months it's a different hospital. In my first year, I rotated to Albury. Jenny was still studying there but, after a few weeks, she went to Canberra hospital for her final year placement. On finishing my three months at Albury, I rotated to Melbourne in May.

I found a good apartment in the city near the Royal Women's Hospital. It was in a nice area with Royal Park nearby for exercise when I had the time. The work was completely different from Warragul. It was a very big hospital and I had three months of night shift.

Every night shift, I covered multiple medical specialties. I would do the paperwork, the examination, and formulate the management plan for any admissions for rheumatology and respiratory cases, along with emergency admissions. Usually, emergency would contact the consultant on call and if the patient was accepted, they would call me to do the admission. If, for example, a patient needed an IV line, I would do it, and if a patient became unwell I'd have to assess them and try to help.

The nights were fun because I got to meet the night doctors. We all knew what twelve-hour shifts were like. A few of them became friends right from my first night: Nazir from Bangladesh and Meena from Egypt. Everyone did their own job but we got to meet up from time to time.

That first night was like a resident's job. At the end of the shift I was asked by medical workforce administration if I'd like to be the medical registrar for three nights because the regular registrar was sick. My new friends were stunned. The first night I was one of them, the next I was their boss. Hilarious!

The registrar's job was incredibly busy – especially for a newbie. MedCalls are medical emergencies where, if a patient in any ward becomes seriously unwell, the nurse will call MedCall as a voice alarm. We all had to run to the patient, and as registrar, I was the leader and had to instruct all staff on what to do. This happened three times in thirty minutes on one shift and was an enormous responsibility.

The medical registrar is also bombarded by the admissions. I had nine in one shift, with every admission taking forty-five minutes to one hour. What an experience – hard but rewarding work. But I was never tempted to accept the position again.

After completing that first year, I moved up to be a registrar. I was rotated to a respiratory unit.

Working with one intern, three registrars and a consultant, I enjoyed the respiratory unit work. I learnt a lot there as the consultant was always asking questions. Surprised that I could always answer him correctly, he commended me and I was pleased that I was making a good impression.

When I joined the Royal College of Physicians, I applied for my previous experience in Iraq and Warragul to be credited; they recognised that as one year and three months. With the nine months at Western Health, I theoretically needed to do only one more year before sitting the exams.

Unfortunately, the director of training wouldn't accept that. Despite not joining a study group and without extra study, I was sure I'd pass. However, if I failed it wouldn't be good for the hospital, so the director said to do the additional year – which was disappointing.

In 2012, I applied for a job at Western Health for the second year and was accepted. A month after commencing, I joined a study group, and with four others, got together every week to prepare for the exams. It was a very good experience and was fun to be studying again.

Reunited with Saleem

In 2011, Jenny finished university and graduated with her degree. We were living together in Melbourne, and she was trying to find work. But she needed to do the English exam to get a permanent residency visa.

Meanwhile, my brother Saleem was in Jordan and every year he had to apply for a new visa there. If he didn't have a job when he applied, they would simply kick him out. So, Jenny suggested that I tell him to apply for a refugee visa for Australia. Strangely, I was embarrassed to ask him because somehow, I thought he'd be offended by my suggestion. Saleem is very different to me. He's pure academia, conservative and respectable. And, apart from that one hour at the airport hotel, I hadn't seen him for seven years. Even before that, I was at the hospital in Baghdad and seldom home so I didn't really know him.

'Just ask him!' Jenny said, so I emailed him, explaining the process and asked if he was interested. He was very interested. Saleem had children, and a deep sense of responsibility for their security and future. I realised that he had no room for ego and pride.

Contacting Darren, my favourite immigration agent, I went to Albury at the end of 2011. Even before this, I'd asked Darren to help one of my friends to apply for a refugee visa, which he obtained. Darren told me that I always gave him a hard time because the stories were so sad and it was emotionally hard for him when he worked on the refugee visas. Well, the stories were, and are, one-hundred percent true. That's why they tugged at Darren's heart.

Explaining Saleem's situation, I insisted to Darren that this time I would be paying the right fee, not the small amount he charged me for my visa. I gave him $3,500, and if he succeeded I would give him another $1,500 to make full payment.

Bringing the evidentiary documents together was emotionally difficult. It didn't make it any easier having done it before. When I saw the hardship, trials and suffering we'd had as a family, the tears flowed again. Saleem may not have considered himself as a refugee but when asked to remember things, his sorrow welled up. I was also aware that most Iraqis have suffered – sometimes more so than we had, but it had become normalised for us.

When I called Saleem, I told him the process was emotionally very taxing and that he might need to be prepared for that. I asked him to think about all the events that happened to him and all the friends who had experienced similar things and who were persecuted.

Saleem is a very intelligent person with a PhD in English. He's lectured for fourteen years in universities in Iraq and Jordan. Sending him a copy of Australia's immigration law, I explained that he had to make sure he ticked all the boxes regarding the definition of a refugee. He understood completely and we began to accumulate the required evidence.

After the war, Saleem had worked with a well-known American journalist. She sent a very strong letter of support for him, voicing her concern for him and his family. With that in the armoury, we put together a strong application and submitted it in Melbourne.

Eight months later, Saleem was called by the Australian embassy in Jordan for an interview. He went with his wife who was studying for her master's degree in English and the interview went very well.

The visa we'd applied for was a Family Sponsored Refugee Visa. This meant that I was responsible for all expenses including travel. I was prepared to do that as I had the money. However, the embassy told Saleem that they would change the type of visa. Rather than being a family sponsored visa, they made it government sponsored. It was unexpected and very welcome because it meant Australia would be responsible for all the expenses. Saleem's wife was pregnant, so travel was delayed for a nail-biting six months until their daughter was born. Finally, they arrived in Australia in June 2012.

Before Saleem and his wife came, I'd rotated back to Albury. Excited, I bought a lot of stuff and arranged everything at my house. It was wonderful picking up Saleem and his family from the airport and taking them there. Nine days later, I had my Australian citizenship ceremony and, because Jenny was away working in Sydney as a physiotherapist, Saleem could come with me and represent my family.

Saleem has a big family so they decided to rent a home ten minutes from me. Three days before Saleem arrived I'd received a call from the Arabic programme on SBS, an Australian television organisation. Before he left Jordan, Saleem had applied for a job with them. I told them he'd arrive in Australia very soon. Saleem contacted them immediately and was offered a job.

The Australian government supported Saleem and his family with furniture and things that made life easy for them to settle. There was also an organisation that came every day to take them around. It didn't take long for them to settle and after only three months Saleem was working. Brilliant.

More exams

In 2013 I sat and passed the third-year theory exam without a problem. If I'd taken it earlier I would probably have passed, but failure would have meant not getting the job at Western Health. It was good to devote a year to studying and the group also helped me to study in a more systematic way. We had three lectures every week via video so these could be watched when I was ready.

After sitting the exam, I went to Iraq. It had been seven years since I'd passed the first exam to gain membership of the Royal College of Physicians in the UK. There was a seven-year expiry date to sit the next and final exam, and if I didn't sit it I'd have to repeat everything. There was a theory exam, similar to the Australian College exam, being held in the north of Iraq, so I applied to take it there.

After spending time with my family, I went north to sit the exam. I passed that one and then came back to Australia to take the clinical one. In hindsight, the timing was wrong because I missed five weeks of training while I was in Iraq.

Starting to practise for the exam, I was then rotated to the Sunshine Hospital, part of the Western but not the main hospital where I was part of the medical team and doing night shifts. Initially, I thought I'd be able to practise at night but, on my first night, I found that all my patients were either unconscious or unable to talk. Most of the patients were also elderly and with dementia and with infections. Talking was out.

The clinical exam has two parts. One part is short cases, where candidates have seven minutes to examine the patient without talking to them and then seven minutes to tell the examiners the diagnosis and the management plan. Then there are the long cases, spending forty-five minutes with the patient and coming up with a plan. It was tough for me. Most of my colleagues were trained in Australia and had learnt the system in medical school. In Iraq,

More exams

the training and case presentations were so different. I had the knowledge, but I didn't have the presentation skills, so it was very challenging.

I didn't like the long cases but to do the exam I needed to have experience with twenty, rather than the three I had. I did a lot of the short cases. There were friends working with me, Steven and Jonathan, who'd also come to Sunshine. When I finished my nightshift, they took me to Footscray and I practised there. It was not easy. The director of training was not happy about my short list of long cases.

Going to Sydney to sit the exam, I thought I'd done well and would pass. I was so upset when I failed. The exam was out of 210 points, the pass mark being 120. I achieved 119.

My third exam was the exam for MRCPUK (Membership of the Royal Colleges of Physicians of the UK) in London. If I passed I would get the degree. I applied for one week's leave from the hospital, but they didn't grant it so I was unable to go. That was the second shock.

The third shock was when I applied for the job at Western again in the September. I didn't get it, even though I'd been sure I would. The director was unhappy with me because I didn't practise sufficiently for the clinical exam; it was a horrible couple of months. I started to doubt myself. I'd failed to get the degree in Iraq to become a specialist. I'd failed the UK one because seven years had passed and I'd have to repeat everything, and I'd failed the Australian clinical exam. What a disastrous run!

The only option I had now was to sit the clinical exam again after one more year of training. There were no jobs available to do that because the hospitals were saturated with staff, so I started to apply for locum jobs. At much the same time, I received feedback from the exam. I had almost achieved a pass with very little practice. That gave me motivation.

With three months of work left on my contract, I was sitting with my consultant when he asked me where I was going the following year. I told him the situation so he spoke to the director, who promised to help me if an opportunity came my way. Then two people dropped off the staff and there were two positions available. I was so happy when the director asked me if I was interested in working at Western again.

That next year, I was very energetic. Not doing very well in an exam isn't a reflection of how good or bad a doctor I am. My exam failure was due to presentation; I had to come to terms with that and overcome it. Australia had a way of presenting that I didn't appreciate until I drilled down into the problem with friends and listened to their tips. One said that I should experience a lot of consultants' methodology, listen carefully to what they say and always ask for feedback.

A health scare

I started with night shift at Western. I was due back at the hospital the following morning when Jenny told me that my eyes were moving strangely. One eye was moving one way and the other eye was moving another way. She asked me to have it checked when I got to the hospital and I told her that it might have been tiredness or my glasses.

Arriving at the hospital, I met one of my friends, Chris, who was in neurology and, while we had coffee, asked him to look at my eyes. I told him that I sometimes saw double, so he had a look. 'Shit,' he said, 'We'd better get you upstairs and have another doctor take a look.'

Within an hour I'd been admitted. The senior doctor diagnosed a problem with one of the nerves to my eye and wanted me in hospital. A consultant gave me even worse news, telling me I had a brain tumour and arranging for an immediate MRI. The consultant was incredibly blunt. He didn't tell me there was a possibility of a tumour, just that I had one. While sending messages to Jenny and Saleem, I began to feel deeply concerned. I lay down in preparation for the investigation. The doctor said that should they see something abnormal they'd inject some dye and do the scan again.

During the long MRI, I took my mind off all the equipment noise by trying to calmly plan the end of my days. Once I got the diagnosis, I would get my bag and go to Baghdad, just to live my last moments close to my family. There was no point in doing anything else. No treatment, nothing. You can't really do anything about a brain tumour. Suddenly the machine stopped and someone came and injected the dye. I thought, 'Oh, my gosh!' I wasn't afraid, but it was upsetting.

A health scare

Around one o'clock, as I was waiting for the results, I went to the computer to access my images but a doctor told me I wasn't allowed. Sometime after five-thirty another doctor appeared and told me that they couldn't find a tumour. No answers yet, but what an enormous relief. I stayed in for three days while I had a barrage of tests. Everyone was good to me and most visitors were my friends.

One of the consultants told me that he thought I'd had a very small stroke. Starting me on aspirin, he discharged me from hospital but said that the problem needed sorting out and referred me to a friend of his, Neil Shuey, a consultant neuro-ophthalmologist at St Vincent's Hospital. He had been an optometrist and then decided to do medicine, choosing to become a specialist. He was very knowledgeable.

By the time I saw him, I was seeing double. Neil told me I needed to take three weeks off work to start the tests. I asked if it would be OK to go to the hospital to do my exam practice; he told me there was no problem. After I'd sent the sick leave form to the hospital director, she saw me there doing practice. 'Aren't you sick?' she asked. I was sure she thought I was up to something dodgy, so I explained what the consultant had said.

That problem took nine months to resolve. I was so impressed with the doctors along the way, and Dr Shuey was a lovely person. Examining me thoroughly, he had me take a host of tests, including a CT scan, and asked me to come back when they were done. After trying to pay for his services at reception, I was told not to worry as the costs were to be bulk billed.

After three weeks, all the tests came back negative. In the meantime, I'd been practising hard, and had started back at work. But I still had double vision.

I did a case with Professor Green, the Head of Oncology, and he gave me very good feedback on how things were done. Before I saw him, I'd done thirteen cases with other doctors and failed every presentation. Professor Green asked me to do another case with him. Doing it the way he taught me, I passed. I began to understand the standard protocol and worked hard at it with two cases a day.

I was very active compared to the previous year. I'd learned my lesson. The good thing was that I understood my mistakes and how I could match the standard, and even go above it. I did six cases with the director, and she was impressed. She realised that not only had I improved, I'd learnt.

*

I had to stop driving. On roundabouts, I would see double and not know which lane to use. It was distressing. Meanwhile, we had practice exams on the weekends and I was failing the x-ray and ECG investigations because we had to look at them from the side where I'd see double. This was not a good way to prepare for, let alone take, the exam.

I went to the director and asked her to help me by submitting a report to the college, requesting that the examiner show me the investigation in front of my face rather than from the side where I was having the double vision. The college accepted and said all the tests would be presented in front. That was a relief because even the loss of one mark could be vital.

Still with that double vision, I went to Toowoomba in Queensland for the exam. Victorian doctors sit their specialist exams in Perth, Sydney or Toowoomba. Doctors from Queensland go to Melbourne or Sydney. We all go to different states for our exams, which I think might be for the exposure to different patients and examiners.

I stayed five days in Toowoomba just to rest and relax a little before the exam. I did well and had no trouble. I was confident that I would pass because I did the presentations according to the standard, and the improved preparation helped.

Once I had finished the exam I would be able to get advanced training. I was interested in doing endocrinology so I attempted to meet all the endocrinology directors in each of the hospitals. Some didn't have time to meet with me but some were able to see me. The head of one of the units at St Vincent's saw my very long CV and asked about my age – that's annoying because they're not supposed to do that. Stating I was thirty-nine, I knew my chances were slim.

Unfortunately, graduating from Iraq was also a disadvantage for me because I was always asked about research, a master's degree, a PhD, or publications – of which I had little. Endocrinology was not an option for me.

Usually the default advanced training is general medicine, and there are many jobs in that area. I applied to Monash, the Northern Hospital, the Alfred, St Vincent's and the Western. I managed to get an interview at all the hospitals except the Alfred. Monash has a very good reputation as a centre for training so I called Dr Bruce

A health scare

Maydom and asked if he could help me. He contacted Monash, but didn't tell me at the time.

I was interviewed by a professor, Dr Richard King, and asked questions including ones about leadership and whether I'd had any leadership roles. I told him that when America invaded Iraq, I ran a hospital of four hundred beds when I was twenty-seven and a medical registrar. He told me that was enough. I got the job. Later on, I met Professor King in Monash Hospital, and reminded him that he'd interviewed me. 'Yes,' he said. 'I remember, you gave me the best answer about leadership.' Being Mr President all those years ago finally paid off!

The Western, where I was still working, called to offer me an interview but I apologised and told them I had been interviewed by Monash and had been accepted there. I like the Western but it's good to have different hospital training and be exposed to different methods.

My eyes were still a problem. I went to see Dr Neil Shuey and found that all the tests including a CT scan of the chest were normal; he didn't find anything. He told me he was starting me on treatment because I might have myasthenia gravis, which is an autoimmune disease that causes muscle weakness. Dr Shuey decided to trial a certain therapy because there were a few conditions that could cause my problem. He wanted to see if the treatment would help. It is a way of doing things sometimes if you are unsure of the condition. He put me on steroids but there was no change.

After six weeks without change, Dr Shuey was worried that the first MRI might have missed a cancer – too small to be detected. He said that after six months we should now be able to detect it if it was there. I was also to have a lumbar puncture which added to my anxiety about the situation.

The MRI and lumbar puncture came back negative and Dr Shuey said that he was referring me to another specialist.

Two weeks later, with Dr Shuey's help, I had an appointment with Professor Lionel Koval. He's the President of the International Strabismus Society, an ophthalmological group, and extremely well known internationally. Walking into Dr Koval's room was like walking into the Middle East – full of Middle Eastern flavour and decor.

Dr Koval asked me where I was from and I told him Baghdad. He asked me if I was Muslim; I confirmed I was. 'Shi'a or Sunni?'

he asked. 'Shi'a,' I replied. He then told me that his father and grandfather came from Abraham and Isaac. In my mind anyone who descended from Mohammed also descended from Abraham. In Shi'a traditions, anyone who descended from Mohammed or Abraham was called sayyid, which means master. They have a very high position in Iraq's Shi'a hierarchy, so I told him that he would be much respected there. Boy, was I dumb. I never thought for a moment that he was actually Jewish.

Dr Koval did two hours of tests and a thorough examination. He printed out two articles from the nineteenth century and demonstrated that there were probably only twenty or thirty cases like mine; it was not a common condition at all and there was very little medical literature about it.

Known as advanced esotropia, it's secondary to myopia. He said that because of short-sightedness, my eyes were not moving to one side and said that every year it might get worse. When the problem reached a measurement of sixteen I would need surgery. At that time, it measured three.

Meanwhile, Dr Koval said treatment would be prism glasses, and sent me to an optometrist in Hawthorn who would do that for me. In the end Dr Koval was the one who worked out what my problem was. He had tested me for two hours. Usually he would charge $570 but he only charged me $170. And everyone up until then had been incredibly generous with their time and had charged me minimally or not at all. Wonderful!

It was amazing. I had nine months of uncertainty and fear before Dr Koval discovered what was going on. I went to the optometrist where he did a lot of tests and then arranged the glasses. When I got them, I could then see things as one, rather than double, from two or three metres away. I haven't tried driving again but it's something I will definitely do. The glasses do not cover the sides of my eyes, so I see double at the side. I just have to turn my head. Eye problems solved.

Monash 2015

I finished at Western and went to Monash. My first six-month rotation was cardiology, because I wanted to improve in that area. If I eventually wanted to work at Warragul where most of the cases were cardiology, I needed more experience. The cardiology department was called MonashHEART.

One of the challenges working there was being the registrar on call. When a patient came into emergency with a heart attack, I needed to be in the hospital within ten minutes. The patient is taken for catheterisation and then we do an angiogram. Then it's on to a lifesaving procedure to unblock the artery. Time is critical because the earlier the patient is treated, the less damage is done to the heart.

At Monash, I had the hospital mobile phone when on call. The hospital could call me at any time – three or four o'clock in the morning. Sometimes another hospital would send a patient by ambulance and would call to say the ambulance would arrive at emergency in ten to fifteen minutes. As I lived on the western side of Melbourne, a one-hour drive from Monash, I decided to rent one room in shared accommodation at the back of the hospital. That way I could just run to the hospital.

MonashHEART, covering an area that included over a million people, was a rewarding and fascinating experience with a lot of innovative intervention. The rural area around Monash is also covered by the hospital, so calls from a GP about a patient having a heart attack came in from time to time. I would oversee the whole process and manage the logistics by mobile phone. I would manage the transfer, get the ambulance, let emergency know, call and tell my consultant the situation, and start running to the hospital.

I really enjoyed the work, and the teaching was comprehensive and happening almost every other day. We attended cardiac conferences where heart surgeons and cardiologists met and examined complex cases – an enriching experience.

My start time was seven thirty but I'd usually be at the hospital by six. The registrars were all in cardiology training and had been doing the job for two or three years. Because I was just starting, I wanted to be at the same level as them in terms of knowing my patients.

I had around twenty patients and was in one of two cardiology teams under a consultant. I didn't want the consultant to feel at a disadvantage because I was a newbie cardiology registrar, so I was going in early at six o'clock to see all my patients to make sure I knew what was going on. I also stayed behind when my work had officially finished. It wasn't a burden because I enjoyed the work immensely and stayed up to speed.

Cardiology was busy. One on-call weekend I received 250 phone calls and had to answer questions about patients or transfers.

Some nights had me returning to the hospital three times for heart attacks – midnight, three o'clock and five o'clock – and then back at the hospital to work from seven-thirty to five.

When I started at Monash, Jenny was three months pregnant and her due date was in my last week there. Being away from Jenny was very hard but she was amazingly supportive and understood the situation. In the last week of cardiology, I was on call, when at eleven at night, I received a call from Jenny in labour. Calling the other registrar to take over on the understanding I'd do an on-call for him the following week, I took off for the Royal Women's Hospital where Jenny had a private room and I was allowed to stay.

Having seen births before, I wasn't concerned about the procedure; it was more about Jenny's peace of mind and fear of the pain. She asked me if the labour would be a lengthy one; I told her not to worry and then quietly prayed to God that it would be swift and with no issues.

Within fifteen minutes, at three in the morning, Maryam was born. I believe that if I ask God for something, God will give to me. Jenny laughed at me and said that even though I was a doctor I was always thinking about asking God about these things. I told her that we had done everything we needed to, the doctor was here, there was good nursing support but she still needed help from God – we all did.

After Maryam was born I experienced something I least expected: confusion and shock. I was in turmoil: there were mixed feelings of joy, happiness, fear, and concern, and so many ideas and thoughts running through my brain. I was overwhelmed with the new responsibility; did I do the right thing bringing a child into this world? And I had silly questions in my head, like whether she would look Iraqi or Korean.

Jenny had a friend visiting, so I went away to have breakfast and to think things through. As it is for many new fathers, it was a very strange feeling. I was about to rotate back to Warragul and only be home on weekends, so I also had to think about our situation. Saleem had gone to his SBS job in Sydney; without family around to support Jenny, it would be tricky.

We stayed at the hospital for two days and we were looked after like hotel guests. They taught us everything about taking care of a baby, so we went home with a bit of know-how and confidence to start looking after Maryam. Fortunately, a Korean friend of Jenny's offered to help when I was away, which was so helpful. It was a great relief to be able to continue my work and not worry about Jenny and the new arrival.

ICU

I spent the next six months at Warragul, after which Monash gave me another year, with the first rotation in ICU (Intensive Care Unit) back in Melbourne. Cardiology and ICU were known as 'A groups' which means acute medicine. ICU was three shifts of twelve hours either night or day and then three days off, which meant I could spend more time looking after Maryam. Jenny also started to go back to work, building towards her own clinic.

ICU is another amazing health service experience. The critical medicine protocols were challenging, and the staff were great to work with. Our teamwork and protocols saved lives. For example, one night during my first time in ICU, a young girl came close to death. It was five o'clock and I was on call with a senior doctor. There was no way to save the patient unless we put her on the heart lung machine to give her an artificial heart.

We started the process by calling the cardiologist and surgeon, and within half an hour the head of cardiology did a heart ultrasound via her mouth – we had organised for the theatre to be prepped. After the surgery that saved her life, the girl was put on the heart lung machine and transferred by plane to the Alfred Hospital where they had the equipment to continue treatment. She was saved by the early intervention and prompt treatment. I felt proud to work with the team. Working in ICU I saw the art of medicine. I realised just how good the health system is in Australia.

Working in the team I managed to form very good relationships with everyone. That's not as easy as it sounds because there can be a lot of competition among those very intelligent people. In cardiology I hadn't seen competition, only teamwork. General medical work is all about the team and how to bring about the best outcome for the patient.

Palliative care

My advanced training for three years was all done, apart from an elective. I could now choose any field I thought I needed training in. I had heard about palliative care, where training leads to a diploma. I had previously done only three weeks filling in for a doctor in palliative care, so my exposure to it was minimal. There is one committee in Victoria which decides about the job and where you go. I applied for palliative care, went for the interview and did well explaining why I wanted to do it.

When I was working in Warragul as a registrar, there was no palliative care consultant. If I needed palliative care input I had to call for advice. With quite a few patients requiring the care, it would have been valuable to have had a consultant to see them. I told the committee that I intended to work at Warragul as a specialist general physician, and that I thought I would be of great value to the community if I had that palliative care training. The committee agreed, and I got the job at Eastern Health.

It was a wonderful experience. I went from A group to C group, which is sub-acute palliative care, and worked at Wantirna Hospital. A small hospital with only thirty-two beds, it doesn't include any acute medicine, it's mainly a rehab unit with palliative care. Leaving at six in the morning, travelling there by public transport took me two hours.

There is so much you can do for patients and their families. There was a music therapist and a spiritual care practitioner. I enjoyed every day that I went out there because I could make a difference in the lives of the patients and their families. It's a great service that the dedicated and passionate team provide and it's much appreciated by the community. But initially, it wasn't all plain sailing.

The first week I was most concerned. The consultant, Dr Kenner, the manager of one of the two teams, was very touchy and would get easily upset during orientation. I wondered how I could possibly last the six months with him, but then I was placed with the other consultant, Dr Sandeep. Incredibly relieved, I found that he had excellent communication skills and was compassionate towards his patients. The patients trusted him, he was knowledgeable, and he was considerate with the staff. Then, five weeks after I'd settled into the work, he told me he'd been offered the position as Director of Palliative Care at Frankston and was leaving.

That was shocking news even though I'd known Dr Sandeep only briefly. When we had the farewell party in the department you could see how upset and sad everybody was, even though we were happy for him. When you have such a valuable, kind and knowledgeable person, it is hard to see them leave.

During those five weeks I learnt a lot, particularly about the meaning of palliative care. The common belief that palliative care is dealing with death isn't accurate at all. In the World Health Organization (WHO) definition of palliative care, the word 'death' isn't mentioned, rather it is trying to improve the quality of life for the patient and their family during a terminal illness, cancer or other illness in its last stages.

The definition of palliative care really concentrates on quality of life. Working in ICU and cardiology where the focus is on keeping the patient alive and doing everything possible, in palliative care we use all our resources to improve the quality of the lives of the patients and their families. That's what I learned from Dr Sandeep and it helped me to have a good base to work from.

I was assigned to another consultant, Dr Lee, but only worked with her for a short time, and then the teams were swapped. I was back with the dreaded Dr Kenner.

Learning more from palliative care

I thought Dr Kenner would be hard to work with, but I was proved very wrong. I soon realised he was a great person. He was knowledgeable, and smart with therapeutics. His palliative care experience spanned something like twenty years and he had developed his use of therapeutics, the drug treatment protocols, into an art. Interestingly, I learned those drug protocols twenty years ago, back in medical school. They're now regarded as old-fashioned because few doctors now know how to get the best out of them. But he did. He knew how to get the best out of every drug he used to alleviate a patient's symptoms.

Every day working with Dr Kenner became a pleasure. Underlying the kindness of his heart and his advocacy for the patient was his determination to make them his priority. I learned from him continuously and began to appreciate the different dimensions to a patient. He calculated everything in relation to the symptoms. Dr Kenner taught me how to visualise the patient from the inside and to try to anticipate what symptoms the patient might experience. I'd never done that before.

Libby was our spiritual care practitioner. Not religious herself, she studied spiritual care. She didn't provide solutions to patients but attended to patients with spiritual needs. For example, a patient may have done or said something bad to someone and in their last days may want to release it from their heart. There may be suppressed anger, bitterness, or something else affecting their spiritual well-being.

When the doctors identified someone who might benefit from a visit from Libby, she would sit with them and become a friend. She did not provide answers or solutions; she'd just sit there, hold their hands, listen and explore what the patient was feeling. She then took whatever anger or distress they had out of the room. That greatly helped our patients begin to find peace.

We had a patient whose husband and daughters had different ways of thinking about what was best for their wife and mother. The husband and doctor were distressed. Libby organised a family meeting with the husband and daughters and they were able to sort it out. From our side, we told them we would focus on the doctor's expert opinion and on what was best for the mother. Telling them they would not have any responsibility on decision-making in that area would relieve the stress on them. Libby spent a long time with them and, in the end, they were content.

Another lady was quite upset with the health system in Australia. Her husband was young, and dying from cancer. When I spoke to her I discovered, not surprisingly, that she wanted to do everything for her husband. Checking the internet, she saw that certain drug trials were happening in America and she wanted her husband on them.

She was disappointed with our health system and thought that our unit would not be able to provide anything for her and her husband. I told her about the spiritual care practitioner that she could talk to, and the music therapist that could help with a music session for her and her husband. I also told her that we had nursing staff that could provide care for her husband. He was incontinent and needed a lot of cleaning and nursing care. I told her we were part of the public system and yet we provided all these things to the community. It made a huge difference to her attitude and expectations. Libby also spent a lot of time with her.

A week later, we started to see the wife smiling and happy as her distress retreated. She had more confidence in the health system and how we were able to help her. A week or two later, her husband passed away but she'd managed to smile and relax a little in his last few days. She told us how much she appreciated our services.

The music therapist was a fantastic guy. Some patients would like to sing, some wanted to write a song for themselves. Some patients were musicians, so he brought instruments in for them. Others just wanted to listen to a certain type of music, so he'd bring in the music of their choice.

Palliative care is often expected to be hard on a patient but it's quite the opposite. The team works every moment, night and day, with the sole purpose of addressing the patient's needs, looking after the families and using medical intervention to relieve symptoms.

Each team had only sixteen patients; we worked nine hours a day so there was plenty of time to do the things that were important. One day I had three family meetings, with each meeting lasting an hour. It's such a difficult time for the patient and their family, and every family has different expectations and needs.

We had entirely new experiences every day too. One lady in her fifties had cancer and had gone through major surgery to relieve her symptoms. She'd been in rehab, but that hadn't helped her, so she was confined to bed and suffered from pain. Crying every day, she simply wanted to go home and spend time with her kids.

Initially, she was unable to move because it caused pain. Dr Sandeep suggested we change the medication to a very strong analgesia. Within two weeks her pain was under control and we could start rehab.

When she graduated to using a walking aid, her friends got her 'L' plates for her walker. Within six weeks we could get her home. In her last week with us she told me about her bucket list – one that she'd made when she first came into our care and knew she had a short time to live. Two of the things on it were having breakfast with her husband and dancing with her son.

I told her that she'd taught me a lot about determination. She was a strong woman and could achieve what she wanted. It was a great experience.

Palliative care hasn't changed my view of death, but it has changed my view of life. Whenever I see my patients, I never talk about death, or what might be after death. I always work in the moment and ensure we make the best of it.

When a patient approaches death, the team doesn't try to hold them back. They take it badly if a patient dies uncomfortably and think they should have done something differently to improve things for them. Sometimes we had patients we'd known for a long time. We got to know them and made a connection. Some patients came to us many times, some patients stayed for weeks and we'd talked to them every day. When they died it was hard on the whole team.

We instituted a self-care programme; every Friday we scheduled a meditation session under Libby's guidance, and encouraged the staff to participate.

Of the enormous range of experiences influencing my life, palliative care has been an opportunity to learn, rather than something that shaped me. The diverse viewpoints were invaluable for incorporating into my medical practice.

I love my job and when a patient recovers it's still an amazing feeling. The patient–doctor interaction creates a special bond. And the more experienced and qualified I become, the more I'm able to relieve pain. Everyone has a story – we know that – but listening to the stories of older patients gives me special pleasure, so I tend to spend more time with them.

Richly rewarded in many ways, I finished palliative care and returned to Warragul in 2017: this time as a consultant.

Postscript

Over ten years ago, Jenny asked me what would make me happy. My reply was that nothing would make me happy because I wasn't pursuing happiness.

That has changed. When I read a particular email recently, I felt immense joy and happiness. In fact, it meant so much to me that I read and re-read the email repeatedly and wept for most of that day.

So, if I wasn't pursuing happiness, what was I chasing all my life? That was a hard question, and I concluded that my life objective was not in pursuit of happiness but living a form of rebellion. Every step of the way.

Existing in poverty in my early childhood, I rebelled against the status quo and started working at age thirteen.

When death cruelly took my sister and crushed me, I rebelled by deciding to become a doctor. I would fight death from the other side. I would stand in its way and battle it head-on. I drew on my rebellious spirit and rose to academic success in a humble high school and then picked up a stethoscope – my weapon of choice.

The academic road to medicine in the midst of war was difficult enough. However, that and the devastating and unjust death of my brother, Naeem, proved the perfect fuel for the rebel doctor. When war came, in the absence of proper government and during the American invasion of Baghdad, I stood firmly for justice, working hard to protect the integrity of the hospital and university, and ensuring that patients had fair access to medical services.

Handing over the hospital to the newly appointed management, I went back to study to make my dream of becoming a specialist come true. As I continued, many of my friends and the people I knew either lost their lives or disappeared. Even sitting exams was life-and-death, as missiles rained down on us. Yes, I was afraid – very much so. But rebels draw on a determination that is close to madness, spurring them on regardless.

In Australia, everything seemed to conspire against my life's quest to become a doctor. But, my spirit was strong, and time and again, the rebelliousness in me surged. I fought the odds for more than ten years to achieve my dream.

I did it. I am here at the other end.

In March 2018, I was admitted as a Fellow of the Royal Australasian College of Physicians (RACP) and became a specialist. My dream came true. I had commenced my training in October 2002 and succeeded in my endeavours sixteen years later.

That email, the one that brought me to my knees in tears, was from the President of the Royal Australasian College of Physicians informing me that I was granted a Fellowship.

Currently a consultant physician at West Gippsland Healthcare Group, I'm part of the Baw Baw Physicians in Warragul and an adjunct senior lecturer at Monash University.

And yes, I am happy. Happiness found the rebel doctor.

About the Author

Issam Muteir graduated from Iraq's Al-Nahrain University (formerly Saddam University) in 2000 and completed his internship and specialist training in Internal Medicine in Baghdad. He completed his training at the Royal Australian College of Physicians in 2017.

Currently Issam is a Consultant Physician at Warragul Hospital, Victoria, and adjunct senior lecturer at Monash University. He is a part-time student at the University of Sydney in his final year of a Master of Medicine (Clinical Epidemiology). He also has a Diploma in Child Health from the University of Sydney.

Rebel Doctor – From Baghdad to the Australian Bush is his first writing experience. A memoir about his life, it is an inspirational and powerful story; it is magical, and it is entirely true.

Trafalgar Sth.

To the Staff on the third floor of W.H.

I wanted to write you a note to say thankyou for your care of me on the 8th 9th 10th December. I am the lady you looked after who IS going to Paris for Christmas, thanks to you all.

The nurses that attended me, were all wonderful, kind and compassionate, with lots of humour thrown in, so we could all have a good laugh — the best medicine —

To the tall and handsome Iraqi Doctor, in his beautiful blue shirts, who treated me with compassion and humour. Life, I would think, has not always been easy for him, and yet he showed such kindness. I wish him well, whether it is here in Aust., or back in his home country, of which he is a true Ambassador.

I have told a number of friends and family, that if I was the Queen of Eng I could not have had better care.

I wish you all a joyous Christmas as we celebrate Jesus birth, and may 2011 bring with it many blessings as you care for those in need, and an extra dose of patience as you deal with over-demanding patients, and those who think it is their roll in life to complain about everything !! I think you are all wonderful.

With kind thoughts of

www.ingramcontent.com/pod-product-compliance
Lightning Source LLC
Chambersburg PA
CBHW021102080526
44587CB00010B/348